VICKY,

ENJOY THE BOOK!

A TASTE OF CORAL GABLES

A Culinary Tour and Recipes from the City Beautiful

Paola Mendez

Books & Books
Press

an imprint of Mango Publishing Group

CORAL GABLES, FLORIDA

ACKNOWLEDGMENTS

The publisher gratefully acknowledges Coral Gables restaurants for their assistance in supplying information and images, and for providing access to their establishments during the research, writing, and photography for this book. The publisher also acknowledges:

- The City of Coral Gables and Vine Communications for making introductions and providing input;
- Paola Mendez for supplying much of the writing and some of the photographs;
- Andrea Mendez for supplying some of the photographs;
- Nabila Verushka for supplying some of the photographs;
- Mike Urban for supplemental writing, editing, photography, and overall project management;
- The staff of Mango Media for general support and project guidance and for supplying production and manufacturing expertise as well as cover design;
- Vicky Shea of Ponderosa Pine Design for text design, page makeup, and overall design guidance.

Contents

Foreword

A few years ago, after my wife and I had moved to Coral Gables, the restaurateur Danny Meyer from New York asked me to suggest one place to eat while he was in Miami for a work trip. The pressure! I went through my mental Rolodex of what was new and hot. The restaurants that immediately came to mind, clustered mostly in South Beach and Wynwood, were very good. But I didn't feel that they were *Danny Meyer good*. So I went out on a limb and pointed him to Eating House in Coral Gables. Open for a couple of years then, some of Eating House's new-restaurant buzz had worn off. But I believed that talented chef-owner Giorgio Rapicavoli was cooking at the top of his game at that moment. He was: Danny loved everything about Eating House and was wowed by Giorgio's creative cuisine.

That memory exemplifies what I love about dining in Coral Gables. We, too, have our share of flashy new restaurants and hotly anticipated openings. But we also have—more than many of our neighboring communities—established restaurants that are acclaimed by critics and beloved by locals. Places like Ortanique, where I know chef Cindy Hutson is going to make me happy with her Caribbean-infused cooking and the best mojito in town. Places like Mikuna, where the Peruvian food is some of the best I've tasted outside of Lima. Places like Palme d'Or, where chef Gregory Pugin's food is served with such exquisite care and hospitality, you feel like a VIP every time. And places like Eating House, where Giorgio's food seems to evolve with changing seasons, tastes, and trends.

Miami is fortunate to have pockets of great dining options in just about every neighborhood. But there's something special cooking in Coral Gables. If you ask me for a restaurant recommendation, it's probably going to be somewhere in The City Beautiful.

Evan S. Benn
Former Food Editor, *Miami Herald*
and Editor-in-Chief, *INDULGE* magazine

Giralda Plaza at night.

Introduction

Coral Gables is a treasure trove of culinary delights. From busy Giralda Avenue and Miracle Mile to the outlying coffee houses and eateries, there's plenty to explore in this vibrant city.

A Taste of Coral Gables is a cookbook and restaurant guide filled with great recipes and colorful descriptions of the City Beautiful's best, most notable food establishments. Organized alphabetically by restaurant, and with a recipes index in back, the book is easy to navigate and fun to peruse.

You'll find many places you're no doubt familiar with, and hopefully some new ones to explore. And the recipes reflect the diverse, multicultural culinary landscape that helps make Coral Gables so special to residents and visitors alike. Enjoy!

Aragon 101

In September 2012, Coral Gables native Erica Guzman opened Aragon 101, a home décor boutique and cooking school in the heart of the City Beautiful. She drew her inspiration from many of the interesting and intimate European shops she enjoyed while living in Milan.

Aragon 101 brings together the best of those concept stores, while adding the distinct tropical flavor of South Florida. Regular cooking classes, together with private dinner parties, allow guests to enjoy delicious food and sharpen their culinary skills in a relaxed setting. There's a variety of international cuisines featured at the dinners.

Guest chefs from throughout South Florida and beyond preside over the cooking classes and private dinners. Diners sit at Aragon's long, white counter in the back of the store and take in a culinary floor show—all while enjoying a glass or two of wine and lots of lively conversation. There's plenty of back and forth between chefs and diners, making Aragon 101 a truly interactive dining experience.

Erica continues to travel to spots near and far, looking for décor items reflecting originality and fine craftsmanship. She believes in doing what you love and sharing that love with others.

GOUGÈRES (SAVORY CHEESE PUFFS)

½ cup water

½ cup milk

4 ounces (1 stick) unsalted butter

Large pinch coarse salt

1 cup all-purpose flour

4 large eggs

1 cup shredded Gruyère cheese, plus more for sprinkling

1 teaspoon Dijon mustard

Freshly ground pepper

Freshly grated nutmeg

1. Preheat the oven to 425 degrees. Line three baking sheets with parchment paper.

2. In a small saucepan, combine the water, milk, butter, and salt. Bring to a boil. Over low heat, add the flour, stirring continuously with a wooden spoon until a smooth dough forms, about 2 minutes. The flour should just begin to coat the bottom of the pan.

3. Transfer to an electric mixer and bowl fitted with a paddle attachment and let cool for a minute. Beat on low speed, adding eggs one at a time. Make sure each egg is thoroughly mixed in before adding the next. Add the Gruyère, mustard, and a pinch each of pepper and nutmeg.

4. Transfer the batter to a large, sealable plastic bag, and snip off ½ inch from one corner.

5. Squeeze 2-teaspoon-sized balls onto the baking sheets. (You may use a small ice cream scooper in lieu of the plastic bag method.)

6. Sprinkle a small amount of cheese on top of each ball, and bake for 15 minutes. Reduce the temperature to 350 degrees and continue to bake until golden and cooked through, about 10 to 15 minutes.

SERVES 6.

Aromas del Peru

Aromas del Peru serves a mix of authentic, delicious Peruvian Creole cuisine with a few innovations and modern takes on traditional favorites. You'll find Peruvian must-haves like Papas a la Huancaina, Lomo Saltado, Pargo Frito, and Churrasco steak. And if you like ceviche, this is a great place to have some. Aromas del Peru offers a range of these popular fresh, raw fish dishes, which are cured in citrus juice.

The Ceviche Clasico gives you the option of fresh fish, shrimp, or a mix of both cured in lemon juice. The Ceviche Cholo Power adds yellow, spicy pepper and calaquita onions to the Clasico dish. Also try the Ceviche Chalaco, a mussels ceviche with spicy rocoto, a Peruvian pepper.

Aromas del Peru is a good choice for any type of gathering, from a family or group of friends to a romantic dinner for two. The restaurant has a rustic feel with white walls, dark wooden furniture and beams, and wrought-iron accents. The terracotta floors and entrance and dark red chairs add a hint of color.

The space is separated into two rooms. The smaller, more intimate room features a bar and several tables, while the main room has a projection screen where soccer matches are televised.

LOMO SALTADO

½ pound steak

1 onion, cut into strips

1 tomato, cut into small
    chunks

1 clove garlic, minced

½ cup chopped cilantro

½ cup cooking oil

2 tablespoons vinegar

2 tablespoons soy sauce

3 teaspoons red wine

    French-fried potatoes

1. Cut the steak in long pieces.

2. Add oil to a medium skillet over medium heat and fry the
   meat until seared.

3. After the meat has browned, add the onion, tomato, salt,
   pepper, and garlic and stir until warmed through.

4. Add the wine, vinegar, and soy sauce and continue stirring
   until blended in.

5. Remove the beef mixture to serving plates. Garnish with
   cilantro and serve over French fries. Serves 2.

Bangkok Bangkok II

Bangkok Bangkok II is an authentic Thai restaurant on Giralda Avenue serving traditional and delicious Thai favorites. Their menu also offers a variety of vegetarian and vegan options.

The restaurant's walls are covered in dark wood paneling highlighted by ornate golden statues and other accents. The restaurant offers four different seating options. The most adventurous option is to sit on the floor on woven pillows around low tables with intricately carved edges. You must remove your shoes to enter this dining area. Definitely try this for the most authentic experience. There is a back room with decorative umbrellas on the ceiling and a front room with a view of Giralda Avenue. Located on Restaurant Row, Bangkok Bangkok II also offers gorgeous outside seating on the stone-paved, pedestrian-only street.

As you walk into Bangkok Bangkok II, you immediately experience the aroma of sizzling grilled chicken satay and peanut sauce. Start your meal with spring rolls served with a sweet and tangy dipping sauce. Order one of their popular specialties: pad Thai, fried rice, sweet and sour chicken, or red curry vegetables. If you still have room, cap off your meal with tempura ice cream and Thai donuts.

CLASSIC PAD THAI

8 ounces flat rice noodles, cooked

1 pound shrimp

2 eggs, lightly whisked

½ cup roasted peanuts, chopped

  Tamarind concentrate

2 tablespoons lime juice

¼ teaspoon cayenne pepper

1 tablespoon fish sauce

2 fresh scallions, thinly sliced

  Bean sprouts

1. Extract the tamarind concentrate. Infuse it with fresh lime juice, cayenne pepper, and fish sauce to form the base sauce for the dish.

2. Heat a large skillet on high to pan-sear the shrimp. Set aside.

3. Fluff the egg mixture in the heated skillet, then add the rice noodles.

4. Sauté the remaining ingredients with the base sauce.

5. Top with bean sprouts.

SERVES 4.

Bellmont Spanish Restaurant

Bellmont Spanish Restaurant serves authentic dishes from Spain made from scratch with the very best ingredients. Originally a restaurant and bakery, Bellmont Spanish Restaurant switched out its bakery for a bar. Now, there's a great selection of wines from various Spanish regions.

The restaurant has a modern-meets-rustic Spanish atmosphere. The lamps and furniture feature sleek, straight lines, and the tables are covered with white linens. In contrast, the bar is made from weathered, dark wood with small trellis details. There are piles of chopped firewood for the oven and a large collection of wine corks, giving the modern décor a warm ambiance while maintaining a level of elegance.

Enjoy a true Spanish feast by starting with delicious tapas. Fried garbanzo beans with a fried egg and chorizo, a Manchego cheese tray, and hand-cut, imported Jamon Iberico and chorizo are the bestsellers. The paella is cooked to order and made with the finest Calasparras rice. Make sure to order it at the same time as you place your appetizer order, as it takes 25 minutes to cook.

Bellmont also hosts flamenco nights with live entertainment and talented flamenco dancers. It's a show not to be missed.

FIDEUÁ

2 pounds thin fideo noodles

1 pound white onions, diced in small brunoise

1 pound green lamuyo pepper, diced in small brunoise

2 ounces smashed fresh garlic

1 pound chicken breast, cut in small pieces

1 pound Ibérico pork loin, cut in small pieces

1 pound fresh Spanish sausage

8 ounces extra-virgin olive oil

2 bottles mild Spanish beer

1 gallon chicken stew

Fresh saffron (una pizca)

Salt and white pepper, to taste

1 teaspoon fresh ground black pepper

Spanish sherry wine (vino de Jerez)

1. This dish is best prepared in a large paella pan.

2. Fry the fideo noodles in plenty of oil until golden and crispy. Remove from the pan and set aside.

3. Add the garlic, onions, and green lamuyo pepper to the oil in the paella pan in intervals of 1 minute over medium heat. Continue with the chicken, pork loin, and Spanish sausage.

4. Once all the meats added are halfway cooked (approximately 12 to 14 minutes), add the Spanish beer. Stir gently and wait until the beer reaches the boiling point.

5. Add the fried fideos and start adding the warmed chicken stew, little by little, keeping the fideos loose, smooth, and tender and not stuck together or to the paella pan.

6. Add salt and white pepper to taste. The fideos are properly cooked once they start curving shapes in the paella pan. Lower the heat to the minimum to eliminate any excess of stew.

7. Let the paella pan rest for 4 to 6 minutes, then add a generous portion of Spanish sherry wine.

SERVES 10-12.

Note: Seafood and peppers may be added a few minutes after the stew is added and placed atop the final dish. Recommended additions: ½ pound shrimp, 1 pound fresh mussels, 1 pound calamari, 2 pieces langoustine, and piquillo red peppers.

Biltmore Culinary Academy

For a magical gastronomic experience, take a cooking class in the beautiful kitchen of the Biltmore Culinary Academy. This recreational cooking school is located inside the historic Biltmore Hotel and offers classes for adults and children. During the class, attendees learn by actively preparing a gourmet meal. At the end of the class, all the students sit and enjoy the dishes they cooked together along with a glass of wine.

The kitchen is a blend of industrial and designer motifs. It's equipped with a professional stove in the center, and designer cabinets line the walls. Open walls in the kitchen are used as chalkboards, where teachers write out important instructions.

The Biltmore's Executive Chef Dave Hackett takes the floor and lays down some ground rules of the kitchen before classes begin. You will learn important pointers, such as how to carry knives around the kitchen safely and keeping your station and floor clean to avoid slipping and accidents.

Then, it's time to start cooking! The participants split up into groups, and each one is assigned a dish. Chef Hackett and several assistants walk around, answering questions, but the students do all the cooking. The menu is always delicious and all the recipes are creations of Chef Hackett.

BLACK BEAN AND FARRO CAKE

1 cup black beans, remove any stones or hard beans, soak overnight

6 tablespoons olive oil, divided

½ cup farro

¼ cup yellow onion, chopped

¼ cup celery, chopped

1 tablespoon fresh garlic, chopped

2 large eggs, beaten

¾ cup coarse fresh bread crumbs

1 teaspoon fresh thyme

¼ cup chopped cilantro

Sea salt as needed

Black pepper as needed

Sliced cherry tomatoes

Spaghetti vegetables (make using a mandolin)

1 medium zucchini

1 medium yellow squash

1 medium carrot, blanched and cooled

1 medium leek

1. Place the soaked black beans in a large saucepan, and cover the beans with two inches of water. Bring to a boil, then reduce heat to low and simmer until tender, about an hour. Remove from heat, season with sea salt, and allow the beans to stand for about 10 minutes prior to draining. Place in a shallow pan and allow them to cool.

2. In a separate saucepan over medium heat, add about a tablespoon of olive oil, then add the farro and lightly toast, stirring constantly, until it starts to brown, about 2 minutes. Cover the farro with water by a couple inches and season with sea salt. Simmer on medium heat until grains have begun to pop open and are tender, about 30 minutes. Drain the farro and place in a shallow pan. Allow them to cool.

3. Heat a small frying pan over medium heat, add two tablespoons of olive oil, add the chopped onions, celery, and garlic, and sauté until the onions are translucent. Season with sea salt and cracked black pepper. Once tender, remove from the heat and place them in a large bowl.

4. Add half of the black beans and farro to the onions, celery, and garlic mixture. Then add the two beaten eggs, coarse bread crumbs, sea salt to taste, and fresh thyme, and mix until well incorporated, adjusting seasoning as needed. Add the remaining black beans and mix in gently to incorporate.

5. Form the black bean and farro mixture into four large patties, cover with plastic wrap, and refrigerate for at least 30 to 45 minutes.

6. Heat a large, nonstick frying pan over medium heat. Add two tablespoons olive oil (more, if needed). Add the patties, and fry on one side until browned and crispy, about 4 minutes. Flip and repeat on the other side. Remove from the pan and set aside.

7. In the same large nonstick frying pan, add one tablespoon of olive oil, add the spaghetti, vegetables, and sauté until hot, season with sea salt and cracked black pepper.

SERVES 4.

PARCHMENT-BAKED ORANGE GINGER WILD SALMON
with Shaved Fennel, Cherry Tomatoes, and Shitake Mushrooms

1. Ask your seafood provider for a one-pound-plus piece of salmon with skin on and scraped, to make sure the scales are removed, and double-checked for bones. Cut into four equal portions.

2. Microplane the orange, cut into segments, and set aside. Keep zest and slices separate.

3. Peel and microplane the ginger. Mix with the orange zest and olive oil to make a paste and set aside.

4. Shave the fennel very thin with your knife, slicer, or mandolin and set aside.

5. Cut cherry tomatoes in half and set aside.

6. Wash and remove the stems of the shitake mushrooms and set aside.

7. Season both sides of the salmon with sea salt and cracked black pepper, then smear a light coating of the orange ginger paste on the flesh side of the salmon.

PARCHMENT POUCH ASSEMBLY

1. Place a piece of square parchment paper on your prep table, and rub the center with a little olive oil.

2. Place about ¼ cup of the fennel in the center of the parchment and place the salmon on top of the fennel.

3. Arrange the vegetables (cherry tomatoes, shitake mushrooms) around the fish.

4. Place three orange segments on top of the salmon, and drizzle with a little olive oil.

5. Grab the corners of parchment, hold them up slightly to form a pouch, and add two ounces of dry white wine to each pouch.

6. Pull all four corners up, twist the bag closed, and bake in a preheated 325-degree oven for 15 to 20 minutes.

7. Carefully open each bag, and garnish with chive spears.

SERVES 4.

4	wild salmon filets, 4 to 5 ounces each
1	cup shaved fennel
1	fresh orange
1	tablespoon fresh ginger
12	cherry tomatoes, cut in half
12	medium shitake mushrooms
12	chives (garnish)
8	ounces dry white wine
4	pieces square parchment
	Olive oil as needed
	Sea salt as needed
	Cracked black pepper as needed

CHEF DAVID HACKETT

Chef David Hackett has been in the hospitality industry for over 35 years. Hackett's experience as executive chef includes many prestigious properties and resorts, including the Westin Diplomat Hotel, Westin Charlotte, Mansion at Forsyth Park, Doral Golf Resort & Spa and the JW Marriott Dubai. He has competed in numerous ACF, Société Culinaire, Geneva Association Culinary Art Salons, and NICA ice-carving competitions throughout his career. Chef Hackett is a professional member of the international food and wine society Chaîne des Rôtisseurs and a lifetime ambassador of the WACS Emirates Culinary Guild.

CHEF GIUSEPPE GALAZZI

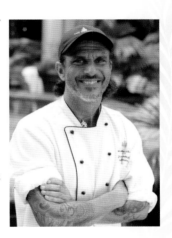

Born in Ferrara, Italy, Chef Giuseppe "Beppe" Galazzi developed his culinary passion from his grandfather, a chef, and began his pursuit of the culinary arts at the age of 14. Heavily influenced by his teachers at the Culinary Institute in Ferrara, Galazzi's curiosity about food grew into the skill with which he now executes every dish. Chef Galazzi attributes his unique style to his love for traveling, absorbing recipes from various cultures and transforming them into his own creations using local and organic ingredients.

ROASTED RED PEPPERS COCONUT PURÉE

2   whole red peppers
½   cup coconut milk
    Sliced cherry tomatoes

1. Using metal tongs, roast the red peppers over an open flame to char the outsides. Place them in a bowl, cover with plastic wrap, and allow to sit for 15 to 20 minutes. Once they are cool enough to handle, peel the skins off of the peppers, remove the seeds, and set aside.

2. In a small saucepan, heat the coconut milk up just short of boiling.

3. Place the peppers in a blender, add half of the coconut milk, cover, and blend. Check consistency and add the remaining coconut milk, if desired.

4. Use as a sauce for the black bean and farro cakes. Garnish with sliced cherry tomatoes.

SERVES 4.

New and Notable in the City Beautiful

FIOLA

Fiola Miami is Fabio and Maria Trabocchi's first restaurant venture outside of Washington, D.C., and it's the Michelin-starred Fiola's second location. The restaurant serves contemporary takes on classic Italian cuisine. Fiola's 8,000-bottle wine cellar is accompanied by a curated mixology and bar program. The restaurant's interior evokes an old-world meets new-world style and is located in the historic 1515 Sunset Building.

HOUSE OF PER'LA

Paul Massard and Chris Nolte of Per'La Specialty Roasters and Giorgio Rapicavoli of Eating House fame recently opened House of Per'La coffee shop, a culinary-driven coffeehouse just off Ponce de Leon Boulevard in the heart of Coral Gables. Serving cold-brew coffees and an eclectic mix of desserts, pastries, and more, this new spot in the former location of Café Curuba is already developing a fanatical local following.

CAJA CALIENTE

Caja Caliente brings a 'tropical y tranquilo' vibe to Coral Gables. Home of the famous Original Cuban tacos chef/owner Monica 'Mika' Leon brings fresh, family recipes to the City. 808 Ponce de Leon.

BACHOUR

Renowned pastry chef Antonio Bachour brings his instagram worthy desserts to Coral Gables in a stunning, 5,000 square foot eatery and workshop space. The menu is Contemporary American, and features a full-line of viennoiserie, egg-based dishes, tartines, sandwiches and salads as well as Bachour's petite-gateux, macarons and bonbons. Serving breakfast, lunch and weekend brunch, the open concept space is also a hub for culinary professionals to perfect their craft, by attending 2 and 3 day workshops with Bachour, who was named Best Pastry Chef 2018. Bachour is located on the ground floor at 2020 Salzedo.

AD LIB

Ad Lib features an all-star culinary team with a focus on modern-American cuisine, rooted in authenticity. Award-Winning Chef/Partner Norman Van Aken and two-time James Beard finalist Executive Pastry Chef Hedy Goldsmith, both Miami natives, will lead the charge to create a special neighborhood gathering place, bringing together locals and visitors alike. Ad Lib will deliver an elevated, yet approachable menu, and dishes will reflect a sophisticated playfulness coupled with a thoughtful approach to responsibly sourced meats, local produce, and wild-caught fish and seafood.

RODILLA

This Madrid, Spain–based sandwich chain is opening its first U.S. outlet on the Miracle Mile this spring. Long known in Spain as an excellent place for fast-casual dining, Rodilla will bring a new level of style and sophistication to the downtown café scene.

Bulla Gastrobar

If you're looking for a fun night full of sangrias, cured meats, and tapas, Bulla (pronounced *Boo-ya*) is the place to go. This Spanish gastrobar is known for its amazing food, chill atmosphere, and super friendly service. Their drinks are also on point.

Start your exploration of Spanish cuisine with white sangrias. Made with white wine, blueberries, strawberries, and blackberries, they are sweet and refreshing—everything you want from a sangria.

Pair your drink with a tray of mixed cured cheeses and pan con tomate. Executive Sous Chef Felix Plasencia recommends Jamón Serrano (Fermin Serrano ham, aged 18 months), Lomo Ibérico (cured Iberian pork loin), Idiazábal cheese (firm sheep's milk, lightly smoked, from the Basque country), and Manchego cheese (three-month-aged sheep's milk). The cheese tray is served with membrillo (a sweet fruit-and-honey jam), walnuts, and cubed pieces of ciabatta bread.

Be sure to try their signature dish, the Huevos Bulla: a jumbo organic fried egg served over homemade potato chips, Serrano ham, and potato foam with drizzled truffle oil. The perfectly fried egg, crunchy potatoes, and creamy sauce taste amazing. If you are a fried egg lover, this is a must.

ENSALADA DE PULPO

16 ounces octopus, pre-cooked

8 ounces heirloom tomato (yellow/dark red colors, diced ¾-inch cubes)

8 ounces Roma Tomato (diced ¾-inch cubes)

16 ounces European cucumber (diced ¾-inch cubes)

2 ounces red onion (fine julienne)

4 ounces extra virgin olive oil

8 ounces lemon juice (fresh)

8 teaspoons dried oregano

4 teaspoons kosher salt

28 croutons

Maldon sea salt

Fresh black pepper (ground)

Olive oil

1. Place the cooked octopus on a hot grill until slightly charred. (*Tip:* Octopus should be just slightly charred; do not overcook.)

2. Remove from the grill and slice into ½-inch pieces. Reserve for plating.

3. Add tomatoes, cucumbers, onions, olive oil, lime juice, oregano, and kosher salt in a small mixing bowl. Toss until everything is evenly coated.

4. Add the croutons and toss one more time.

5. Add the salad mixture to a serving bowl. (*Plating tip:* Pile high by building a base and stacking a couple of pieces from the salad mixture at a time.)

6. Place the grilled octopus on top of the salad.

7. Garnish with Maldon sea salt, fresh ground black pepper, and olive oil. (*Tip:* Add just enough dressing to make sure the salad is not dry.)

SERVES 4.

WINE PAIRING
La Crema Monterey Pinot Noir Rosé.

Café at Books & Books

Coral Gables has the one of the best independent bookstores in the country, Books & Books. This bookshop is so much more than a book retailer. It has been a pillar of the community for over 30 years and has brought revolutionizing events to South Florida, including the Miami Book Fair. This nonstop literary machine hosts events year-round, bringing in all kinds of authors to speak and sign books.

Inside this amazing book-lover's haven, you'll find the Café at Books & Books, helmed by local celebrity chef Allen Susser. When you sit in the half-booths lining the café's walls, you're surrounded by books and a mosaic of photographs of famous authors who have visited the bookshop. You might also bump into a well-known local author working on his or her manuscript. The café and bookstore surround a lovely courtyard with outside seating. It also hosts monthly farm-to-table dinners.

Chef Allen has crafted a sustainable and healthy menu featuring locally grown produce. The menu includes wonderful salads, grilled cheese, quesadillas, and vegetarian options. They also offer a delightful appetizer happy hour on Fridays and live music on the weekends. It the perfect place to enjoy a delicious meal surrounded by books and book lovers.

KEY WEST PINK SHRIMP TOAST

½ teaspoon fennel seeds

1 tablespoon olive oil

12–15 Key West shrimp

½ teaspoon sea salt

½ teaspoon crushed red pepper flakes

1 teaspoon aged sherry wine vinegar

3 tablespoons hummus

2 baguette slices, freshly toasted

8–10 organic arugula leaves

½ teaspoon smoked paprika

7–8 Cilantro leaves

TO PREPARE THE SHRIMP

Heat a small sauté pan and toast the fennel seeds lightly until they become aromatic. Add the olive oil and shrimp. Cook over high heat for 2-3 minutes until the shrimp turn pink throughout. Season with salt and pepper flakes, then deglaze with vinegar. Remove from heat.

TO PREPARE THE TOAST

Spread the hummus evenly on the toast. Arrange the arugula leaves on the hummus. Spoon the warm cooked shrimp over the toast. Sprinkle with smoked paprika and garnish with fresh cilantro leaves.

SERVES 2.

Caffe Abbracci

For nearly three decades, Nino Pernetti and his team have been serving both old friends and new from his beloved Coral Gables restaurant, Caffe Abbracci. The list of regulars reads like a who's who of Miami's movers and shakers. Over the years, they have served countless professional athletes, politicians, including three U.S. presidents, and county, state, and federal judges, including two U.S. Supreme Court justices.

At Caffe Abbracci, everyone who walks through the door is treated like a celebrity and served flawlessly executed Italian comfort food, great wine, and well-made cocktails. You'll find an old-school Italian restaurant atmosphere with chandeliers lighting Caffe Abbracci's main dining room. It's a great place for celebrations, couples dining, or business meetings. You'll usually find a mix of these festivities taking place at the restaurant on any given night.

The menu features traditional Italian dishes, including prosciutto, buffalo mozzarella, risottos, chicken Parmesan, lobster ravioli, fettuccine Alfredo, and veal scaloppine porcini. Start your meal with Tortellini Tatiana stuffed with pear and cheese and served with a pink vodka sauce. Enjoy a tiramisu for dessert with coffee for a perfect ending to your fine Caffe Abbracci dining experience.

LAMB CHOPS WITH DRIED CHERRIES AND BERRIES

11 tablespoons extra-virgin olive oil, divided

1¾ cups Cabernet, divided

1 tablespoon minced fresh thyme, plus 1 teaspoon

16 2-ounce lamb chops, pounded slightly

½ cup mixed dry cherries and berries, plus 2 tablespoons for garnish

4 medium shallots, thinly sliced

1½ cups shiitake mushrooms, stems discarded, caps thinly sliced

1½ cups beef stock

½ tablespoon honey

2 tablespoons minced fresh Italian parsley

Arugula, for garnish

Salt and pepper

1. In a glass or ceramic bowl, whisk 4 tablespoons olive oil with 1 tablespoon Cabernet and 1 tablespoon thyme and season with salt and pepper to taste. Pour the marinade over the lamb chops and refrigerate for 5 hours, turning occasionally. Soak the cherries and berries in 1 cup Cabernet for 1 hour; drain.

2. In a saucepan, heat 2 tablespoons olive oil until hot but not smoking. Add the shallots and mushrooms and cook over moderately high heat about 2 minutes. Add the stock, 1 teaspoon thyme, and the remaining wine to the saucepan and bring to a boil over high heat. Boil until partially reduced, about 4 minutes. Add the honey, parsley, and drained fruit. Lower the heat and cook for 3 minutes. Strain the sauce through a fine-mesh sieve, pressing on the solids with a wooden spoon.

3. Remove the chops from the marinade and pat them dry with paper towels. Season with salt to taste. In a large skillet, heat the remaining oil over high heat until hot but not smoking. Add the chops and cook for about 4 minutes a side for rare. Remove the chops from the skillet and drain the oil from the skillet. Pour the sauce into the skillet and cook over high heat, scraping the bottom of the pan until reduced slightly, about 2 minutes. Season with salt and pepper to taste.

4. To serve, divide the sauce evenly among four warmed plates, reserving some for garnish. Place four chops on each plate. Dot each chop with sauce and garnish with a berry and arugula.

SERVES 4.

Caffe Vialetto

A self-described Italian fusion restaurant, Caffe Vialetto is renowned for its excellent, innovative food and service. With a charming and romantic atmosphere, it's the perfect spot for a tête-à-tête. The restaurant features white tablecloths, fresh flowers, captivating artwork, and an intriguing mix of modern music, giving it a relaxed yet upscale ambience. The staff is attentive and kind and offers high quality service, making sure every aspect of your Caffe Vialetto experience is memorable.

Caffe Vialetto serves up unique and flavorful Italian-influenced dishes like its highly regarded champagne risotto. This dish comes in lamb or chicken teriyaki versions. They also offer broad and varied menu selections, from fried calamari with a chili glaze to creamy polenta, mac and cheese, carbonara risotto, short rib croquettes, and numerous fresh fish and shellfish dishes.

The Caffe is perhaps best known for its bold, innovative pasta dishes. One of the most popular is the pear ravioli, served in a creamy sauce. Vialetto's extensive wine list is sure to have the perfect pairing for your dish. Just ask.

Order the dulce de leche and Nutella panacota for dessert to cap off your fine-dining experience at this renowned restaurant.

Christy's

Christy's, the city's premiere steakhouse, has become a South Florida institution, where you'll consistently find great food and excellent service. This old-school meatery offers an intimate atmosphere with its romantically lit, wood-paneled dining rooms, mahogany tables, and gold-gilded framed paintings. Patrons dress up when visiting Christy's to enjoy a classy, fine-dining experience. It's the perfect place for a business meeting over drinks, and it also offers a superb setting for a special occasion. Christy's bar area is also a popular after-work, happy-hour destination.

Start with the Caesar's salad, a Christy's tradition served with crispy romaine hearts, house-made rustic croutons, and fresh-grated parmesan cheese. For entrées, order one of their top-quality steaks, like the filet mignon or the rib eye steak that's been dry-aged and pairs nicely with a side of mac and cheese.

Dessert highlights include the baked Alaska, made with Neapolitan ice cream that's served over chocolate pound cake, topped with a soft merengue, then drizzled with schnapps, which is set on fire for a flambé finish. Other delicious dessert options include key lime pie, bread pudding, and a brownie à la mode.

This steakhouse is one of the most emblematic restaurants in the city.

Chef Sucre Café

Chef Sucre Café is a petite French bistro with a delectable Latin twist serving brunch all day—every day. This cozy café is located in downtown Coral Gables next to the historic City Hall building on Biltmore Way.

The café's culture is firmly rooted in the local community. Chef Antonio is well known in the area, with more than eight years of experience working as an executive chef in renowned local restaurants like Cacao, Caffe Vialetto, Crazy About You, and Love is Blind.

Chef Sucre Café offers delicious coffee, pastries, and lunch menu items perfect for a quick breakfast or afternoon bite. Stop by for a cafecito break and order a delicious cappuccino or café con leche with a chocolate croissant or a slice of Nutella cheesecake. On a rainy day, try the half-sandwich lunch with a cup of the soup du jour. Sucre is famous for their Croque Madame—a ham and cheese sandwich served in a delicious baguette and topped with a fried egg.

The café's interior offers an inviting atmosphere. A black-and-white mural with the look of chalkboard art graces the main wall. The tables have a wooden-top look and feel, and the chairs are colorful and comfortable, encouraging customers to linger.

BOLOGNESE ZUCCHINI BOATS

3 medium-size zucchinis

ITALIAN BOLOGNESE SAUCE

1 tablespoon olive oil

1 medium white/yellow onion, finely chopped

2 celery stalks, finely chopped

1 medium carrot, finely chopped

3 cloves garlic, minced

2 tablespoons tomato paste

1 can or 8.5 ounces green peas

2 pounds ground beef or turkey

2 teaspoons kosher salt

½ teaspoon dried thyme

½ teaspoon dried oregano

½ teaspoon freshly ground black pepper

⅛ teaspoon ground nutmeg

1 cup whole milk

1 cup red wine

1 28-ounce can whole peeled plum tomatoes

1 bay leaf

1. Line foil over an 8" x 13" or other baking pan. Lightly spray with some no-stick cooking oil or baking spray.

2. Slice the zucchinis in half, and scoop out some of the insides of each half to make room for the Bolognese sauce. Set zucchinis aside on the baking tray.

3. Heat the olive oil in a large pot (preferably a cast-iron Dutch oven) over medium-high heat until shimmering. Add the onion, celery, and carrot, and cook, stirring frequently, until the onion is translucent and all the vegetables have softened, 6 to 8 minutes. Add the green peas, garlic, and tomato paste. Cook until the garlic is fragrant, about 30 seconds.

4. Add the beef or turkey, breaking it apart with your spoon and cooking until it is just browned. Stir in 1 teaspoon of the salt along with the thyme, oregano, pepper, and nutmeg.

5. Stir in the whole milk and bring it to a rapid simmer. Continue simmering until the milk has reduced completely and very little liquid remains, about 10 minutes.

6. Stir in the wine and simmer again until reduced completely, about 10 minutes.

7. Add the tomatoes, reserving the juices, and mash them into small pieces.

8. Add the bay leaf to the pot and stir everything together. The mixture should have a thick, saucy consistency. If it looks dry, add a little of the reserved canned tomato juices until it looks sauce-like.

9. Cover the pot and cook on low heat for 6 to 8 hours. In the last 30 minutes of cooking, check the sauce. If it looks soupy, remove the lid to allow any excess liquid to evaporate. If it looks a little dry, stir in some white wine. The finished sauce should be thick and creamy.

10. Stuff each one of the zucchinis generously with the sauce. Apply a layer of shredded mozzarella cheese, and bake in a preheated 350-degree oven for 15 minutes.

SERVES 4 TO 6

Chocolate Fashion

Chef Georges Berger, owner of Chocolate Fashion, bakes the finest French pastries in all of South Florida. It doesn't matter what you get at this French bakery/restaurant, it will be fresh and fantastic.

Chocolate Fashion is perhaps best known for its weekend brunch. The eggs Benedict has fresh Hollandaise sauce made from scratch. The pancakes are enormous and fluffy, with different flavors like chocolate, banana, and blueberry. The French toast is made from Chocolate Fashion's famous brioche bread and is one of their bestselling brunch dishes.

The local professional crowd enjoys having lunch at Chocolate Fashion. Every weekday, the restaurant features a wonderful lunch special that often sells out quickly. By offering just one lunch special, Georges can offer unique, affordable, super-fresh cuisine. He buys just enough fish for the lunch rush and once it's sold out, that's it. The next day he may buy enough meat to make churrasco for his lunch rush, and once it's sold out, he's done for the day. Each day, a completely new meal is offered, keeping the menu surprising and varied. You can eat lunch at Chocolate Fashion every day for a couple of weeks before seeing the same dish twice.

CHOCOLATE FASHION LEMON TART

12 ounces butter, cut into small cubes

6 ounces sugar

16 ounces all-purpose flour

1 egg

1 teaspoon pure vanilla extract

LEMON CURD

3 ounces lemon juice

Grated zest from 1 lemon

4 ounces egg whites

1 egg yolk

2 ounces sugar

4 ounces butter

1. Preheat the oven to 325 degrees.

2. Mix the butter, sugar, and flour well, then knead the resulting dough lightly. Set aside in the refrigerator for at least one hour.

3. Sprinkle some flour on the counter or table, and roll the dough to ¼-inch thickness. Arrange in a tart mold, and bake to a light brown color, around 12 to 15 minutes. Set aside to cool.

4. Scale the ingredients in separate containers.

5. Put a bowl in a bain-marie on medium heat, pour in the lemon juice, and add the sugar, stirring with a whisk.

6. Add the grated lemon and eggs. Whisk slowly and continuously until it coagulates into a cream.

7. Incorporate the butter and mix until fully incorporated. Pour into the tart shell, and refrigerate for three hours.

CHEF GEORGES BERGER

Georges Berger was a 13-year-old boy living in Lyon, France, when he decided school was not for him. He quit and became an apprentice at the local bakery. After only three years, he received his first pastry chef certification. When Georges first arrived in the United States, he worked for Celebrity Cruises as a pastry chef. He dreamed of opening a French bakery, and in 2004 he found the perfect location in downtown Coral Gables. He felt confident about opening Chocolate Fashion in the South Florida city with the highest concentration of French residents. Chocolate Fashion has become a neighborhood gem treasured by locals of all nationalities.

Copper 29 Bar

For a night on the town, make sure to add this hip spot to your itinerary. Copper 29, a speakeasy bar with a modern twist, is a nod to the golden age of cocktails.

You'll find a dark wood bar accented with vintage wallpaper, chandeliers, and what appears to be old-fashioned portraits on the walls. On closer examination, the paintings feature pop culture figures such as Elvis Presley, Silvester Stallone, and Michael Jackson, each decked out in historic military garb. The front of the bar area features big, comfortable couches and floor-to-ceiling windows that open up onto the new pedestrian walkway on Miracle Mile. When you sit and enjoy your food or drinks in this front area, it feels like you're sitting outside.

The cocktail and food menus go along with the creative, comfortable atmosphere. Truffle mac and cheese is a Copper 29 favorite with white cheddar, fontina cheese, crispy pancetta, and toasted breadcrumbs. Pizza lovers go for the short rib flatbread with gorgonzola cheese, pear, and figs. As for drinks, try the copper mule, margaritas, mojitos, or one of Copper 29's signature cocktails made by the bar's master mixologists. You won't be disappointed.

COPPER 29 SHRIMP AND SCALLOP CEVICHE

2 pounds raw shrimp, peeled and roughly chopped

1 pound raw sea scallops, quartered

1 quart fresh lime juice

10 Serrano peppers, seeds removed, then minced

1 bunch cilantro, rough chopped

1 15-ounce can coconut milk

2 tablespoons kosher salt

2 whole red onions, julienned fine

Plantain chips

Combine all the ingredients (except the chips) in a large bowl and allow to marinate for 3 hours in the refrigerator. Serve with the plantain chips on the side.

SERVES 6–8.

CraveClean Protein Bakery

CraveClean is a bakery specializing in delicious, guilt-free goodies, including cookies, cupcakes, brownies, cake pops, and donuts. It's the place to go to enjoy a treat without derailing your diet or compromising your healthy life-style.

Owner Francesca Morello was tired of eating protein bars with ingredients she didn't recognize. So she decided to experiment in her kitchen, baking with whey protein instead of flour. The result is an array of baked goods that are gluten-free, high in protein, free of refined sugars, and low in calories.

The cozy bake shop is clean and inviting, with dark wood floors and hand-lettered chalkboards. The staff is friendly and conversant in their menu offerings, ingredients, and baking processes. They offer coffees and espressos with an array of milk substitutions that pair perfectly with the healthy baked goods.

If it's your first time visiting, try the carrot cupcake, chock full of little pieces of carrot and chunks of walnut. It's sweet with hints of cinnamon and topped with a thick, smooth cream cheese frosting. The red velvet cupcake with cream cheese frosting is another favorite. Their moist cake pops taste like lightly baked brownie batter. If you prefer local flavors, order the guava cupcake. It sells out quickly almost every day.

CRAVECLEAN PROTEIN-BASED ALMOND COOKIES

½ cup almond flour

⅓ cup vanilla or chocolate protein

½ teaspoon baking soda

1 teaspoon chia seeds

2 tablespoons stevia

2 tablespoons slivered almonds

4 tablespoons liquid egg whites

1 tablespoon coconut oil

1. Preheat the oven to 350 degrees.

2. Measure out and place all the dry ingredients into a bowl, then add the wet ingredients.

3. Mix all the ingredients together until combined to a sticky consistency.

4. Spray a baking sheet with nonstick spray, and divide the mixture into eight equal parts.

5. If desired, add more slivered almonds, some chocolate chips, sprinkles, nuts, or whatever your palate likes, and form each part into a ball using your hands. (You may wish to spray your hands with nonstick spray.)

6. Place the balls onto the baking sheet, spaced evenly, and flatten them gently with your hand into the size cookies you'd like.

7. Bake in the preheated oven for around three minutes. Keep an eye on them. They won't change color much, but they should be soft and easy to lift off of the tray.

8. Let them sit for a few minutes to cool down before serving.

MAKES 8 COOKIES.

Cibo Wine Bar

Hailed as one of the top five wine bars in Miami, Cibo Wine Bar serves authentic Italian fare to lovers of fine wines. Located right on Miracle Mile, this restaurant is the perfect spot for a relaxed lunch or a special night out.

Just like their menu, the restaurant's décor offers a mix of classic and modern. Upon entering, you encounter a large, stylish room with vaulted ceilings and a bar in the center. The back wall is covered from floor to ceiling with wine bottles. If you order a bottle from an upper shelf, a "wine angel" server reaches it by being hoisted with a harness and wires to fetch it.

Further in, the space transitions into a rustic room with weathered brick walls and wooden butcher-block tables overlooking the pizza oven. The dim lighting glows warmly on the walls, giving the effect of dining in a candlelit wine cellar.

What to order at Cibo? Try their fresh, oven-baked pizza with its thin, crispy crust. And you can't go wrong with the pasta dishes or lobster. Cibo also offers a brunch buffet with a spectacular spread including everything from manchego cheese to Nutella waffles, all fortified with unlimited mimosas.

Crema Gourmet

Crema sprang into existence through a love of coffee and a passion for healthy food. The espresso bar café serves salads, gourmet sandwiches, breakfast, and coffee the European way, using high-quality Italian espresso beans and brewing techniques. The café's name is a reference to the creamy foam that you find on the finest espressos.

Crema set up their Coral Gables shop inside the historic 169 building on Miracle Mile. The décor is industrial chic with superb chalk signage and murals. The walls are covered with subway summer tiles, and the counters are made of rustic, natural wood. The wood furniture adds further to the warm, welcoming atmosphere. With plenty of inside and outside seating, the location is a great place to hang out.

Crema also welcomes customers' furry friends. They will bring a bowl of water for your pup or feline while you sit outside and enjoy your meal or coffee. It's also a great place to read, work, or study. Wi-fi is free, and there are comfortable chairs begging you to stay and hang out for a while. They also offer free infused water—one of many perks to make your visit as pleasant as it can be.

Delicatessen Patagonia

Inspired by traditional tastes from Argentina, Delicatessen Patagonia is a restaurant and market on Miracle Mile. It's the perfect place to stop for lunch after a morning spent exploring downtown Coral Gables.

Inside, the walls are covered with greenery and exposed, weathered brick. Most of the seating inside are half-booths with a long, leather, tufted couch lining the wall, giving the space a warm ranch feel. You can also sit outside, where the tables are right on the new promenade of Miracle Mile. It's a great place for people watching and enjoying the hustle and bustle of downtown Coral Gables.

Known for empanadas, Delicatessen Patagonia bakes their traditional Argentine versions with pastry dough and fills them with various combinations of beef, pork, and chicken. Other recommended menu items include steaks, gourmet sandwiches, and sausages.

For decades, Argentina has been exporting its superior quality beef, known for its natural and unique taste worldwide. At Delicatessen Meat Market, you will find some of the best Argentine meat cuts in South Florida. You will also find a wide selection of the finest Argentine wines.

BAKED SALMON WITH SOY SAUCE AND GINGER

SOY SAUCE DRESSING

- 3 tablespoons low-sodium soy sauce
- 2 tablespoons olive oil

  Salt and pepper, to taste
- 1 teaspoon grated fresh ginger
- 1 teaspoon garlic, finely chopped

SALMON

- 8 ounces salmon filets

  Chopped green onions (for serving)

SOY SAUCE DRESSING

1. Cut and chop two cloves of garlic.
2. Add the soy sauce, olive oil, and ginger.
3. Add the salt/pepper to taste.
4. Stir together all the ingredients.
5. Cover and refrigerate for two days.

SALMON

1. Preheat the oven to 450 degrees.
2. Place the salmon fillets in a baking dish.
3. Pour the soy sauce dressing over the salmon.
4. Bake in the preheated oven for 8 minutes.
5. Serve immediately, topped with chopped green onions.

SERVES 2.

Divino Ceviche

Nestled among some of the city's greatest restaurants along Giralda Avenue, Divino Ceviche is a refreshing break from traditional Peruvian restaurants. It's a casual spot that serves Peruvian dishes with a modern twist.

Upon arriving, a wavy sculpture illuminated with colored lighting greets you with a cool techno feel. The walls have giant murals done in paint and chalk, and the dining area and bar are open, airy, colorful, and inviting.

Start your dinner with tequeños de lomo saltado. These deep-fried, breaded sticks stuffed with steak stir-fry are delicious. They are served with Huancaína sauce, a spicy cheese concoction for dipping.

For your main course, check out the namesake Divino Ceviche, made with fresh fish, avocado, mango, calamari, and shrimp marinated lightly in lime juice, chili, and fresh cilantro. It is served garnished with sweet potato and choclo (Peruvian giant corn).

Another recommended main dish is the Lomo Saltado, a Peruvian beef stir-fry made with onions, tomatoes, cilantro, soy sauce, and garlic, served over rice and accompanied by a side of french fries.

CEVICHE SALMON APALTADO

7 ounces salmon filet, cubed

2 ounces lemon

1 teaspoon coriander

1 teaspoon garlic paste

1 Aji limo chili pepper, blended

1 tablespoon onion, julienned

1 ounce fish stock

1 avocado

1 teaspoon white onion, cubed

1 teaspoon celery

Salt and pepper to taste

1 cubed sweet potato, fried corn, or cubed potato for garnish

1. Cut the salmon into small dice cubes, place in a bowl, add the salt, pepper, and garlic, and stir for 20 seconds.

2. Add the lemon juice and coriander, stir for 10 seconds, drain and reserve liquid in bowl.

3. Remove the salmon and refrigerate.

4. For the avocado purée, place 1 avocado in the blender with the celery and white onion, a few drops of water, and a few drops of lemon and liquefy.

5. Add the avocado purée to the lemon juice reserved in the bowl, add the fish stock slowly to reduce the acidity, and mix well so that there are no lumps.

6. Spread the purée on a plate, stack the salmon cubes on top in the form of a pyramid, and garnish with sweet potato in cubes, the fried corn, and more sweet potato or the potato on top.

SERVES 2.

THE OWNERS

Divino Ceviche is owned by two Peruvian brothers, Frank and Christian Encalada. They were both born in Lima, Peru, and raised in el Doral in the Miami area. Christian studied at the Cenfotur School of Peruvian & International Gastronomy, one of Peru's oldest and most renowned culinary schools. While Christian delved into the world of cooking, Frank studied management and the restaurant industry in the United States. The first Divino Ceviche opened its doors in 2011. The restaurant was an instant success, allowing them to open their second location in Coral Gables in 2013.

CORAL GABLES LANDMARKS

Beautiful and historic Coral Gables City Hall, featured here at night, was a major element in the plan of George E. Merrick, founder of Coral Gables, to create a Spanish-Mediterranean city. The building is three stories tall, built of local limestone, and features a central, three-stage clock tower.

At the intersection of Seville Avenue and Granada and DeSoto Boulevards, DeSoto Plaza and Fountain is one of the numerous plazas, entrances, and fountains that add to the charm of Coral Gables. The fountain, built in 1925, is considered to be of neo-baroque style and features four face carvings that contain water jets and vintage lanterns that cast a beautiful golden hue at dusk.

Built in 1924, the Alhambra Water Tower has been described as a "lighthouse that has never seen the sea." It was built for George Merrick's first platted subdivision north of Coral Gables and was used for storage as part of the water supply system for the city from 1926 to 1931.

Eating House

For a unique, phenomenal gastronomic experience, be sure to check out Eating House. Chef Giorgio Rapicavoli has garnered an incredible reputation for his restaurant, which serves creative modern versions of American fare. Every dish on his menu boasts rich flavors, uses original combinations, and tastes consistently outstanding. At Eating House, everything you order is a handcrafted work of culinary art.

Kick off your Eating House experience with the heirloom tomato appetizer. This light and refreshing dish features nuoc cham (Vietnamese fish sauce vinaigrette), peanuts, nitrogen-frozen coconut milk, and herbs.

When it comes to entrées, the pasta carbonara and the chicken and waffles are bestsellers for a reason. Decadent and delicious, the carbonara is made with black truffle, Applewood bacon, egg yolk, and pepper. The chicken and waffles uses free-range organic chicken, candied bacon, maple syrup, hot sauce, and buttermilk waffles.

Eating House is also known for its Sunday brunch, which features Coca-Cola ketchup, Captain Crunch pancakes, braised pork calentado, and eggs benedict carbonara. Don't miss this top-rated gem of a Coral Gables restaurant.

PASTA CARBONARA

8 ounces Applewood bacon, cut into ½-inch pieces

4 ounces Grana Padano, grated

4 egg yolks

4 ounces heavy cream

1 pound pasta, preferably fresh

Salt and pepper to taste

4 tablespoons black truffle paste

1 cup toasted bread crumbs

1. Heat water in a large pot over high heat. When the water starts to steam, add salt and cover the pot.

2. Heat two tablespoons of oil or butter in a large sauté pan over medium heat. Add the bacon and cook, stirring occasionally, until crisp around the edges, 7–10 minutes.

3. Once crisp, add cracked fresh pepper to the bacon fat, and toast for 30-45 seconds. Add the heavy cream to the pan, bring to a boil, reduce the heat, and simmer for 1-2 minutes. Add the Grana Padano and combine until the cheese has melted into the sauce. Set aside.

4. Cook the pasta until al dente (slightly toothsome), usually 1 minute shy of cooking time if using boxed pasta. Remove the pasta from the boiling water, and add to the bacon sauce. Mix well, adjust the seasoning with salt, and add the egg yolks to the pasta. Combine well, and adjust consistency with pasta water if needed. Finish with the truffle paste, topping with toasted bread crumbs and additional grated Grana Padano.

SERVES 4.

Fontana Biltmore

Fontana, the most romantic restaurant in Coral Gables, is located on the first floor of the beautiful, historic Biltmore Hotel. A gorgeous fountain takes center stage in the restaurant's lush courtyard brimming with plants and palm trees. Dine al fresco in this elegant and romantic setting, where you may also enjoy the Biltmore's towering Mediterranean architectural accents that surround the courtyard.

The restaurant's lovely interior features an open kitchen, where you may see Chef Beppe Galazzi prepare his Italian masterpieces using local and farm-fresh ingredients. You'll find authentic northern Italian cuisine, such as house-made pastas, wood-oven pizzas, grilled meats, and super-fresh seafood. Everything on the menu is superb, especially the chicken parmigiana, seafood risotto, and veal scallopini.

The Fontana hosts Biltmore's famous and extravagant Sunday brunch. The decadent affair includes live music; a breakfast station serving freshly made eggs, French toast, Belgian waffles, and omelets; a seafood station featuring caviar, crabs, shrimp, ceviche, octopus, and oysters; an Italian station; a Japanese station; and a broad array of desserts. The brunch also includes bottomless champagne bellinis, mimosas, and bloody Mary's. Fontana is the height of fine romantic dining in Coral Gables.

PASTICCIO DI MACCHERONI ALLA FERRARESE

BESCIAMELLA SAUCE

- ½ cup (1 stick) butter
- ½ cup unbleached all-purpose flour
- 4 cups hot milk
- Fine sea salt
- Ground white pepper

FILLING

- ⅓ cup dried (or frozen) porcini mushrooms
- 2 tablespoons butter
- 1 cup fresh peas
- ½ cup minced onions
- 1 pound cooked pennette rigate
- ½ cup grated Parmigiano Reggiano cheese
- Grating of nutmeg and truffle oil

MEAT RAGU SAUCE

- 1 celery stalk with leaves, washed and quartered
- 1 large carrot, scraped and quartered
- ¼ cup flat-leaf parsley
- 1 medium onion, peeled and cut into quarters
- 1 tablespoon butter
- ½ pound ground pork
- ½ pound ground chicken
- ½ pound sausage
- 1 teaspoon fine sea salt
- Ground black pepper

BESCIAMELLA SAUCE

In a large saucepan, melt the butter over medium-low heat; do not let the butter brown. Whisk in the flour and cook it until a uniform paste is formed and no streaks of flour remain. Slowly whisk in the milk in a steady stream. Cook about 10 minutes, stirring slowly until the sauce coats the back of a wooden spoon. Season with salt and pepper. Set aside until ready to assemble filling.

MEAT RAGU SAUCE

1. Soak for 15 minutes and drain the porcini mushrooms, if dry. (If frozen, dice them.) Melt the butter in a medium-size sauté pan, stir in the onions, and cook just until the onions soften. Add the mushrooms and fresh peas and cook 1 to 2 minutes. Transfer the mixture to a large bowl and set aside. Return the sauté pan to the stovetop.

2. Mince the celery, carrot, parsley, and onion together. Melt the butter in the same sauté pan used to cook the mushrooms. Stir in the celery mixture and cook over medium heat until it softens. Stir in the pork, sausage, and chicken, season with salt and pepper, and cook, stirring often, until the meats turn gray. Transfer the ragu to the bowl with the mushrooms. Stir in the besciamella sauce. Add the cooked penne rigate, toss the mixture well, and add the truffle oil. Set aside.

PUFF PASTRY

1. Preheat the oven to 375 degrees. Butter a 10 x 13-inch spring form pan. Procure 1 pound of prepared pastry dough and divide in half.

2. On a lightly floured surface, roll out each half of pastry dough into a 16-inch diameter. Fit one half of the dough in the pan, bringing it up the sides and letting the excess hang over the edge of the pan.

3. Spread the filling on top of the dough, sprinkle the cheese over the top, and cover with the second sheet of dough. Seal the edges.

4. Brush the top with egg yolk. Cut a small "x" in the center of the top for venting, and bake for 40 to 50 minutes or until the crust is nicely browned. Cool for 30 minutes before serving.

SERVES 4 TO 6.

Fratellino Ristorante

At Fratellino Ristorante, you're family. As you walk into the intimate Italian restaurant, owner Beto DiCarlo personally welcomes you with a hug and a contagious smile. The family-owned-and-operated Italian eatery opened on Miracle Mile in 2015, serving exquisite Italian fare, and it has built a loyal local following.

DiCarlo comes from a long line of Italian chefs and restaurateurs. The menu consists of the best items the DiCarlo family has served in South Florida over the last three decades. The cuisine is a mixture of southern and northern Italian influences.

Start with the burratina—creamy, fresh mozzarella with prosciutto, black olives, and large tomato slices drizzled with an aged balsamic glaze. The rolled eggplant with ricotta cheese, mozzarella, and a home-made marinara sauce is also fantastic. Even picky eaters who are skeptical of eggplant will enjoy this appetizer.

For entrées, order the ricotta cheese gnocchi with a four-cheese sauce and crispy gratiné. The gnocchi are shaped like scallops and melt in your mouth. The Chilean sea bass risotto, another good choice, features lobster and shrimp with crunchy asparagus.

There's an excellent selection of Italian and Napa Valley wines in a variety of styles and price ranges to accommodate all tastes and budgets.

EGGPLANT ROLLATINI

2 large, thin eggplant slices

1 egg

1 cup flour

½ cup cooking oil

Salt and pepper

2 thin tomato slices

2 small scoops ricotta cheese

½ cup roasted red peppers

¼ cup grated Parmesan cheese

½ cup tomato sauce

2 slices fresh mozzarella cheese

1. Preheat the oven to 350 degrees. Crack the egg in a bowl and scramble. Spread the flour on a plate. Dredge the eggplant slices through the egg and flour, shaking off the excess. Salt and pepper to taste.

2. Heat the cooking oil in a pan over medium-high heat. Once heated, gently place the breaded eggplant slices in the pan and cook until golden on each side, about 2 to 3 minutes. Remove and place the slices on paper towels to drain.

3. In a shallow, oiled baking dish, place the eggplant slices. Top with the tomato slices, ricotta, roasted red peppers, Parmesan, tomato sauce, and mozzarella. Place in the preheated oven and bake for 5 to 10 minutes, until the cheeses melt. Remove from the oven and allow to cool.

SERVES 2.

Fritz & Franz Bierhaus

If you're a soccer fan, Fritz and Franz Bierhaus is the place to watch big games. It was recently voted the number one place to watch soccer in South Florida. They are also known for their block parties celebrating St. Patrick's Day, Oktoberfest, and Blues Fest. During these events, they fill their courtyard with food stations, bars, and a stage for live bands.

Fritz and Franz serves hearty German cuisine and features over 20 different German and Austrian beers. Order the Wurst Sampler or a giant pretzel with mustard sauce for an appetizer. Visit them on a Monday when they offer their famous two-for-one schnitzels: breaded, deep-fried pork or veal served with potato salad on the side.

Fritz and Franz has the feel of a gregarious sports bar, with wood-paneled walls, long communal tables, wall displays of beer bottles, and sports memorabilia hanging throughout the space. There's a stage with signed guitars hanging on the walls. For those who enjoy sitting outside, there are nice biergarten-style tables in the courtyard. Inside or out, this is a great place for beer, soccer, live music, and lively conversation.

BIERHAUS POTATO SALAD

4 large Idaho potatoes

1 medium white onion, chopped

¼ cup scallions or green onions

⅛ cup parsley, chopped

Salt

Pepper

½ cup vegetable oil

½ cup apple cider vinegar

Splash of rice vinegar

1. Cook the potatoes with skins on until soft. Set aside.

2. When cool enough to handle, peel the potatoes, then slice into bite-size chunks.

3. Add the chopped onion, scallions, parsley, vegetable oil, apple cider vinegar, salt, pepper, and rice vinegar.

4. Mix well while the potatoes are still warm. Refrigerate.

SERVES 4.

Gastronomicom

Improve your gourmet cooking skills and discover new recipes at Gastronomicom. This French culinary school offers various cooking programs for students in all different stages of their culinary journeys, from beginners to seasoned pros. You receive the highest standard of cooking, baking, and pastry instruction during your participation in any Gastronomicom program.

Weeklong recreational cooking programs are offered for those looking to learn new recipes, cooking tips, presentation skills, and a general knowledge of French cooking. If you want to take your culinary skills to the next level, there are more intensive programs with durations of one, two, or three months. These programs offer one-star Michelin-level training. Each week revolves around a specific meal course, such as cold starters, hot starters, fish dishes, and meat dishes.

For those looking to take their culinary careers even further, there is a one-year program with three months of training in Miami, three months in residence at the Gastronomicom school in southern France, and a six-month internship at a Michelin-star-level restaurant in France. No matter your level of culinary skill or interest, Gastronomicom has something for everyone who is passionate about fine cooking.

POACHED OYSTERS WITH PORK BELLY AND WATERCRESS SOUP WITH GARLIC FOAM

OYSTERS

2 fresh oysters, unshucked

WATERCRESS SOUP

1 ounce pork belly or bacon

1 ounce watercress

1 tablespoon olive oil

½ ounce potatoes

1 ounce onions

1 clove garlic

1½ ounces cream

3 ounces water

salt and pepper to taste

ALMOND FOAM

1 tablespoon soy lecithin

¼ cup almond milk

2 tablespoons cream

Salt and pepper

Smoked cardamom

1 clove black garlic

1 clove elephant garlic

GARNISH

1 yellow beet

1 dirty squid

salt and pepper

Smoked parika

Lime zest

1 kaffir leaf

BEET CONFITS

1 beet root

1 tablespoon white balsamic vinegar

1 cup sparkling water

Olive oil

Lime

Lemon zest

1. Open the oysters and remove the meat. Reserve the liquid in the refrigerator.

2. Sweat the pork belly or bacon dices, then the onions and the potato dices. When a nice caramel color is achieved, add the garlic and season well. Add the watercress and all the liquid. Cook for 10 minutes on high heat. Blend and strain, then chill in the refrigerator.

3. Put the almond milk, cream, salt, pepper, garlic, and smoked cardamom in a pot and bring to a boil. Add the soy lecithin and blend. Remove from heat, place in the refrigerator to cool, and blend again before serving.

4. Clean the squid and remove the cartilage. Make a juice with the beet and seasonings, then add the squid to marinate. Just before serving, stir in a frying pan for 2 minutes over high heat.

5. Cut the beet into a small dice. Put all the ingredients in a pot and cook slowly for 1 hour until the beets are soft and shiny.

ASSEMBLY

Place the oysters in the shells. Add the almond foam, garnish, and beet confits, and serve with the chilled watercress soup.

SERVES 2.

Graziano's Restaurant

In 1962, 18-year-old Mario Graziano opened a butcher shop in Buenos Aires, Argentina. By 1989, he had 11 butcher shops around the city. He decided to sell all of his businesses and move to Miami in 1990, where he opened his first Graziano's butcher shop on Coral Way and 87th Avenue. It was a true "carniceria Argentina." Now the Graziano family runs four restaurants and five markets in the greater Miami area.

Mario and his wife, Maria Graziano, run the family establishments with their son, Leo, and their daughters Cecilia and Carolina. In 2005, the family opened Graziano's restaurant on Giralda in Coral Gables and then the market on Galiano. The upscale restaurant specializes in fire-pit cooked meats slowly rotisseried with Quebracho wood—or as Leo calls it, "carne al asador." Upon entering the restaurant, you are greeted with a view of two wood-fired grills at work behind floor-to-ceiling glass. Empanadas are Graziano's other specialty.

If you are a wine lover, you definitely must visit Graziano's. The dining room is lined with floor-to-ceiling shelves filled with wine bottles. They stock over 1,500 types of wines from all over the world with a focus on their beloved wines from Argentina.

Graziano's Market

Located just off restaurant-crazy Giralda Avenue, Graziano's Market offers the best of both worlds: wonderful home-cooked foods and baked goods for dining in or carry out, and lots of fresh meats, produce, and wines for cooking and entertaining at home.

The market's main entrance on Galiano Street is flanked by several stylish high-top wooden tables and matching chairs for al fresco sipping and dining. Enter the market, and you're treated to a bake shop, a Panini stand, a steam table loaded with an amazing variety of empanadas, and a butcher counter for fresh Argentinian meats. Scattered throughout the friendly open space are floor-to-ceiling shelves of fine wines. There's also a refrigerator case loaded with fresh fruits and vegetables and a well-stocked grocery section containing specialty foods from Argentina.

The market has morphed into a popular spot for those on the go to grab a quick snack or meal. Numerous tables are scattered throughout the interior space, and flat-screen televisions provide entertainment and the latest news for diners and shoppers alike. There's a tempting menu that features fresh fruit, crepes, French toast, and Argentinean steak for breakfast and specialty paninis, hot and cold appetizers, and meal-sized salads for lunch and dinner.

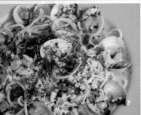

Gusto Fino

Gusto Fino, the best authentic Italian deli and café in Coral Gables, serves hearty, large-portioned subs, pastas, and hot dishes. Any time you stop by, you will most likely find Tony, the owner, sitting at a table making sure the eatery runs smoothly and you get impeccable service.

This local favorite originally started in a little location on Le Jeune Road, but with the enormous demand for the deli's delicious sandwiches, it quickly outgrew the space. Gusto Fino is now on Alhambra Plaza in a spacious location that has ample seating and a long counter perfect for ordering take-out.

Gusto Fino traces its roots to a region in southern Italy known as Campania. The menu reflects the region's simplicity and richness. Gusto Fino specializes in hand-made meatballs, slow-roasted meats, fresh herb dressings, and made-from-scratch lasagna.

A go-to place for lunch, Gusto Fino has won many of the locals over with their famous Sicilian meatball sandwich. Sweet potato fries are the ideal side for this hot, cheesy sub. Another favorite on the menu is the warm chicken Parmigiana sandwich—a lightly breaded chicken breast slathered in Pomodoro sauce and mozzarella cheese.

SICILIAN MEATBALLS

4 pounds Angus ground beef (80 percent lean)

4 eggs

16 ounces plain bread crumbs

1 cup grated parmesan cheese

½ cup diced garlic

½ cup chopped Italian parsley

1 tablespoon kosher salt

1 tablespoon black pepper

1. Preheat the oven to 350 degrees.

2. Mix the bread crumbs into the ground beef.

3. Add all the remaining ingredients and fold in until well mixed.

4. Roll out the meatballs in 3-ounce portions. Use water to help form them, if needed.

5. Place meatballs on a greased sheet pan.

6. Bake in the preheated oven for 20 to 30 minutes, or until the internal temperature of the meatballs reaches 165 degrees.

7. Remove from oven, and allow to cool before serving.

MAKES 12 THREE-OUNCE MEATBALLS.

House Kitchen & Bar

House Kitchen & Bar is a new restaurant in Coral Gables owned by the operators of Town Kitchen and Bar in South Miami. They serve global comfort foods with a focus on fresh local seafood and make the best rotisserie chicken in town. This mixed-fare restaurant also makes a point to support the local community while keeping their dishes as organic and free-range as possible.

Start your dining experience at House with Stracciatella: Homestead-grown baby heirloom tomatoes served over Mimmo's Stracciatella mozzarella. It comes with a side of Zak the Baker toast drizzled with a balsamic glaze.

For your main dish, order the rotisserie free-range chicken. It's tender and full of flavor, and it's served with cornbread, curry mustard sauce, barbecue sauce, and Nashville hot sauce. Chef Altman brines each chicken overnight for 24 hours, marinates them in special rubs for an additional 24 hours and only roasts chickens as needed. The birds are practically cooked to order to keep them as fresh as possible.

House offers outside tables and a lounge with benches and low tables. It's the perfect setting to sit back, relax and enjoy a meal or drink with family and friends.

ROTISSERIE CHICKEN

2 whole chickens, trussed

CHICKEN BRINE

8 quarts cold water

2 cups kosher salt

1 pound brown sugar

¾ cup whole garlic cloves

1¾ cups sliced shallots

2 jalapeños, chopped

4 bay leaves

8 sprigs thyme

1¼ tablespoons black peppercorns

½ tablespoon cumin seed

½ tablespoon fennel seed

CHICKEN DRY RUB

1 cup brown sugar

1 cup all-purpose seasoning or Sazon seasoning

⅛ cup black pepper

1 cup lemon pepper

2 tablespoons cayenne pepper

1 tablespoon curry powder

2 cups paprika

½ cup chili powder

CHICKEN BRINE

1. Combine all ingredients in a large pot and bring to a boil.

2. Simmer 20 minutes.

3. Strain and cool completely.

CHICKEN DRY RUB

Combine all ingredients and reserve.

1. With butcher's string, tie the chicken so that the legs and wings are tucked tightly against the breast.

2. Place the chickens in a deep container, leaving approximately two inches of space above the chickens.

3. Pour the brine over the chickens until submerged. Cover and refrigerate for 24 hours.

4. Pour off the brine, and place the chickens on a drying rack.

5. After 30 minutes, generously rub the chickens all over with the dry rub mixture.

6. Place the chickens back on the cooling rack and refrigerate another 24 hours.

7. If using a rotisserie machine, skewer the chickens and place the breast in. Cook at 140 degrees for 40 minutes to an internal temperature of 165 degrees. If using a grill, skewer the chickens and roast on medium heat for approximately 1 hour to an internal temperature of 165 degrees. If using an oven, place a pan of water on the bottom of the oven to create steam to help keep the chickens moist. Cook the chickens at 325 degrees for 1 hour and an internal temperature of 165 degrees.

8. After the chickens have reached the proper internal temperature, let them stand for 10 minutes before carving.

SERVES 4.

John Martin's Irish Pub

A Coral Gables icon, John Martin's Irish Pub has reigned on Miracle Mile for nearly 30 years. Established in 1989 by lifelong friends John Clarke and Martin Lynch, this relaxed watering hole offers extensive beer and whiskey selections as well as comfort foods.

Upon entering, you're surrounded by a warm and inviting pub atmosphere with a 20-foot-long mahogany bar, wooden floorboards, and large-scale furniture and fixtures from a church in Ireland. The walls are decorated with historic black-and-white photographs, and there's a unicorn stained-glass art piece hanging by the bar.

The front of the pub has a raised platform where you'll find different forms of live entertainment: karaoke, open-mic nights, live music, and trivia nights. Sit at the bar and watch a game on the TVs; or sit at a table and enjoy a classic Irish shepherd's pie—ground sirloin topped with mashed potatoes and cheese. Other bestsellers include the bangers and mash and the Guinness beef stew. Don't forget to order dessert from an array of tasty options, including warm Irish whiskey bread pudding. Being an Irish pub, John Martin's hosts the biggest St. Patrick's Day party in town with ongoing live music throughout the day and night.

JOHN MARTIN'S SHEPHERD'S PIE

4 pounds ground sirloin

1½ large onions, chopped

2 carrots, chopped

6 celery stalks, chopped

2 ounces garlic, chopped

2 tablespoons mixed herbs (fresh or dry)

4 ounces all-purpose flour

6 ounces tomato paste

8 ounces green peas

Salt and pepper to taste

16 ounces water

3 pounds mashed potatoes

Jack and cheddar cheese, shredded

1. Place the sirloin in a heavy-bottomed pot. Add the water and bring to a boil, reduce heat.

2. Pound the meat to prevent lumping, then simmer until the fat is extracted from the meat.

3. Skim off the fat.

4. Add chopped vegetables to the pot and cook for 10 minutes.

5. Stir in the flour, tomato paste, and seasoning, and allow to cook for 20 minutes

6. Add the peas and remove from heat.

7. Allow to cool.

8. Fill pie bowls with beef to 3/4 full.

9. Put a layer of mashed potatoes on top.

10. Cover with cheese and warm in a 300-degree oven for 20-30 minutes.

SERVES 8.

Kao Sushi & Grill

This Japanese–Latin American fusion concept recently opened its doors on Miracle Mile. The restaurant's eclectic, electric décor reflects the unique combinations of flavors you find on the menu. The walls are backlit with a strong blue light, while the ceiling's recessed neon-pink lighting gives an elegant nightclub glow. Rounded booth seating is featured throughout the restaurant. A moving glass door that opens onto Miracle Mile on cool weather days separates the outside seating.

The menu is a combination of steak, fish, pasta, and fried rice dishes as well as sushi with Latin American flavors. If you're not in the mood for sushi, try the teriyaki salmon seared and glazed in teriyaki sauce, sea salt, and lime. Another recommended main course is one of the chaufa rices, a Peruvian-style rice wok dish.

For sushi lovers looking to experiment with Latin flavors, order the Huancaina roll–cooked shrimp and avocado, half covered with salmon, Peruvian huancaina sauce, sesame, cilantro, and crispy sweet potato.

Kao Sushi & Grill also has live jazz bands playing during happy hour when you'll also find discounted sushi rolls and cocktails.

WOK CHAUFA

FOR COOKING SHRIMP

- ⅓ pound shrimp, cleaned, without tails

  Pinch of kosher salt

- ½ cup white wine

- ½ cup mash of garlic, parsley, canola oil, salt, ajinomoto, sriracha, paprika, and lemon juice

- 2 tablespoons canola oil

FOR SAUTÉING VEGETABLES AND RICE

- 1 ounce red bell pepper, finely diced

- 1 ounce yellow bell pepper, finely diced

- 1 green onion, cut in thin rings

- 1 ounce white verdeo wine

- 1 grated garlic clove

- 1 teaspoon grated ginger

- 1 hard-boiled egg, sliced

  Pinch of kosher salt

  Pinch of white pepper

- 2 tablespoons canola oil

- ½ pound cooked rice

- 1 tablespoon soy sauce

  Dash of sesame oil

FOR COOKING SHRIMP

1. Take a pan, let it heat well, and place canola oil to seal the shrimp with the salt.

2. Once sealed, add the white wine and cook until the alcohol evaporates.

3. Turn off the heat, add the mash, and mix with the remaining heat in the pan. Remove and set aside.

FOR SAUTÉING VEGETABLES AND RICE

1. Take a wok, bring to medium heat, add the oil along with the red bell pepper, yellow bell pepper, and green onion, and cook until the vegetables are tender.

2. Add the grated garlic, grated ginger, salt, and ground white pepper. Mix well.

3. Plate the sautéed vegetables, cooked rice, the soy sauce, the sesame oil, and the shrimp.

4. Garnish with the hard-boiled egg and green onion.

SERVES 2.

WINE PAIRING
Hartford Russian River Chardonnay.

La Dorada

La Dorada is an upscale Spanish restaurant specializing in top-quality seafood and Mediterranean Spanish dishes. Much of the fresh fish featured on La Dorada's menu is flown in from the Mediterranean Sea, the North Atlantic, and the Cantabrian Sea. La Dorada's traditional Spanish stews, many of them seafood-based, are legendary on the Coral Gables dining scene.

The restaurant has a nautical atmosphere with polished brass portholes and seascape paintings decorating the walls. The servers wear navy blue uniforms reminiscent of smart-looking sailor suits. Located on the new, pedestrian-only, stone-paved Giralda Avenue, La Dorada also offers a lovely outdoor dining experience at stylish tables shaded by bright, white umbrellas.

The chefs at La Dorada use the highest quality organic, natural ingredients in all their cooking. For openers, be sure to try some of Andalucia's Fritters—various seafoods fried in first-press extra virgin olive oil.

The restaurant's signature dish is its sea-salt-crusted sea bream (dorada). You'll also find specialties from different regions in Spain, such as deep-sea lobsters from Motril, spider crabs from Rias Baixas, and shrimp from Malaga and Sanlucar.

MEDITERRANEAN TUNA WITH FRESH TOMATILLO SAUCE

10 ounces fresh tuna

2 ounces extra virgin olive oil

Salt to taste

TOMATILLO SAUCE

1 ounce extra virgin olive oil

½ teaspoon ground garlic

½ cup tomato sauce

1½ ounces white wine

Fresh chopped parsley to taste

½ cup fresh tomato, chopped

1. Preheat an outdoor grill to high.

2. Sauté the garlic with the extra virgin olive oil.

3. Add the tomato sauce and the white wine.

4. Finish with the chopped parsley and the tomato. Set aside.

5. Put the tuna on the grill, and cook for 3 minutes on each side to medium or medium rare. Remove from the grill, and spoon the tomatillo sauce on top.

SERVES 2.

Lan Ramen-Ya

Take a break from the hustle and bustle of downtown Coral Gables at Lan Ramen-Ya, one of the newest eateries in town. Located on Alcazar Avenue, this magnet for foodies captures all the traditional Japanese styles and flavors of ramen soups and more.

Ramen is a Japanese dish with Chinese influence. It features pasta-like noodles served in chicken or pork broth. You'll find both options available at Lan Ramen-Ya. Their broths are boiled and simmered for hours to achieve intense, complicated flavors.

Order the Classic Ramen-Noodle Soup, with a dense, white-pork broth known as "tonkotsu." They also use a lean pork belly "chashu" for a less fatty version. These ramen-noodle soups are topped with a soft-boiled egg seasoned with soy sauce, bamboo shoots, nori, and scallions. It's a perfect comfort meal for rainy days.

There are also several fried rice menu items worth checking out. (Lan Ramen-Ya's fried rice is a little stickier than traditional Chinese fried rice.) Go for the "Special" version, a bowl of fried rice with shrimp, chasui pork belly, mushroom, spinach, and scallions topped with a fried egg. Be forewarned, it's super heavy and filling, as are the ramen soups. No one leaves Lan Ramen-Ya hungry.

YAKISOBA (JAPANESE STIR-FRIED NOODLES)

1 package pre-cooked
yakisoba noodles
(contains 3 noodle
packets), or ½ pound thin
spaghetti

4 tablespoons grape seed
oil, divided

2 large cloves of garlic,
minced

½ large onion, sliced thin

1 4-ounce package shiitake
mushrooms, cut into thin
strips

¼ head small cabbage, cut
into large dice

1 medium carrot, peeled
and cut into julienne
strips

1 pound flank, strip, or skirt
steak cut into thin strips
against the grain

2 scallions, cut into 1-inch
pieces

3 tablespoons red
shredded ginger
(optional)

Green powder nori
(optional)

SAUCE

4 tablespoons sugar

4 teaspoons soy sauce

2½ tablespoons oyster sauce

2½ tablespoons ketchup

4 ounces Worcestershire
sauce

1. If using yakisoba noodles, put the noodles into a colander under the faucet and run water over the noodles to loosen the bundles.

2. If using thin spaghetti, drop the spaghetti into a pot of boiling water and cook until al dente. Drain the noodles and cool under running water. Put the cooled noodles into a bowl and set aside.

3. Put all the sauce ingredients into a bowl, and whisk until sugar is dissolved. Set aside.

4. Heat a large 12-inch skillet or wok over medium-high heat. Add 2 tablespoons of oil and the beef. Brown the meat on all sides, stirring occasionally, for 2 to 3 minutes. The meat should not be fully cooked. Add the garlic and cook until fragrant, another minute. Transfer to a bowl.

5. Return the pan to the heat and add 2 tablespoons of oil. Add the onions and carrots and cook for 2 to 3 minutes until the vegetables are slightly wilted. Add the cabbage and continue to cook for another 2 minutes. Add the scallions and mushrooms and cook for another minute.

6. Add the noodles and the sauce to the pan. Mix the ingredients gently in the pan and cook for approximately 2 to 3 minutes. Add the beef back into the pan and gently stir, checking seasoning and adding salt or pepper as needed. (The noodles should have absorbed most of the sauce, and the vegetables should be cooked but still firm.)

7. Mound the noodles onto a plate, making sure that the beef and colorful vegetables are visible. Serve immediately, topped with optional garnishes.

SERVES 4.

Le Provençal

Le Provençal has been bringing a bit of southern France to Miracle Mile for over 30 years. It's a "French-style" restaurant: a contemporary ode to the past, combining a bit of tradition with a bit of the new. The menu gives a nod to French provençale cuisine while adding the flair of local flavors and foods. Yet nearly all the dishes are infused with the standard cooking ingredients used in southern France: olive oil, citrus, lots of broths and lighter stocks, and plenty of fresh vegetables and seafood.

The restaurant also has culinary influences from Portugal, Italy, Greece, Spain, and northern Africa. For example, try the North African grilled chicken with a pomegranate glaze and couscous. The Mediterranean grilled halibut is served with a saffron Pernod sauce and a fricassee of crab and shrimp; the salmon comes bathed in a French-inspired sorrel sauce.

You'll also find a bit of Florida passion fruit, le cochon a la naranja, in what is known in Miami as a cochinito: confit of pork with crispy skin and an orange glaze.

Grab a café-style outdoor table beneath Provençal's expansive, shady canopy on Miracle Mile, and enjoy all this delightful eatery has to offer.

COQUILLETTE AU JAMBON, COMTE ET TRUFFE

1 pound macaroni pasta

½ pound jambon de Paris ham, diced

2 ounces Grana Padano cheese, grated

4 ounces Comte cheese, cubed

8 ounces chicken blonde stock

2 large cage-free eggs, yolks

1 cup heavy cream

1 teaspoon carpaccio truffle

2 fluid ounces clarified butter

Sea salt and ground black pepper, to taste

1. Boil the pasta in salted hot water until al dente. Set aside.

2. In a separate stock pot, add the butter, then sauté the ham until golden brown.

3. Add the chicken stock and reduce by half. Add the pasta and stir the pasta with the ham.

4. Bring down the heat to medium.

5. In a separate bowl, whip the cream and egg yolks, then add to the pasta, stirring rapidly. Add the cheese. Mix well, until the mixture coats the pasta.

6. Season with salt and pepper. Garnish with the truffle slices and truffle oil.

SERVES 4.

LOUI

LOUI brings a bit of flair and a lot of charm to Miracle Mile. This restaurant serves Mediterranean-inspired food made with fresh, high-quality ingredients.

A renowned interior designer from Argentina owns LOUI, and it shows. The lovely restaurant is decorated with impeccable taste, giving it a chic atmosphere. There's a mix of lounge and dining room seating, the walls are covered with contemporary art (much of it available for purchase), and the easy-going atmosphere makes you feel right at home.

LOUI is known for its friendly service, and it starts with the owner, whom you'll usually find front and center or roaming the dining room, recommending a menu item or a bottle of wine. The menu offers light yet satisfying options, like their quinoa salad with arugula, red grapes, cherry tomatoes, and pecans drizzled with a Dijon sauce. LOUI regulars always recommend the crab cakes as an appetizer. As for entrées, try the porcini-dusted scallops, the black linguini with seafood, beef lasagna, lobster ravioli, or mushroom chicken. Their varied and flavorful dishes make a wonderful use of exotic spices and natural ingredients.

LOUI RACK OF LAMB

12 lamb ribs

Salt and pepper to taste

Rosemary

1 cup cooked couscous

1 green pepper, chopped

1 red pepper, chopped

1 yellow pepper, chopped

1 large onion, sautéed

1 tablespoon olive oil

1. In a pan, sauté the peppers with the olive oil. Salt and pepper to taste.

2. Mix with the sautéed onion, and prepare the couscous.

3. Cook the lamb ribs on a grill at 325 degrees on each side for 2 minutes or longer, to taste.

4. Spoon the peppers and onions onto plates, arrange the ribs around or on top of the vegetables, and serve the couscous on the side.

SERVES 2.

CORAL GABLES LANDMARKS

The Venetian Pool (above) was created from a coral rock quarry in 1923. The 820,000-gallon pool is fed with spring water from an underground aquifer. In the spring and summer seasons, the pool is filled and drained daily.

Giralda Plaza, the "restaurant row" of Coral Gables, featured the colorful Umbrella Sky Project installation (left) during the summer of 2018.

Coral Gables is home to some of the most beautiful trees in the metropolitan Miami area.

The Miracle Mile of Coral Gables (left) is the beating heart of the city, with its restaurants, shops, hotels, and newly enhanced streetscape.

Madruga Bakery

Madruga is an artisan bakery that also offers breakfast, lunch, and coffee. It's a friendly, warm gathering place where people can meet, have coffee, enjoy a meal, and take home freshly baked bread and other baked goods.

Tall windows give Madruga a sun-splashed interior space. Youthful owner/baker Naomi Harris is passionate about bread, so Madruga Bakery offers a lot of naturally leavened loaves. A mill on site allows the staff to freshly mill whole grains.

Try ordering their popular breakfast egg sandwich. It's very rich and made with a fried egg on a fresh-baked onion poppy roll and stacked with bacon, sautéed kale, cheddar cheese, and aioli. For lunch, their sweet potato sandwich is a standout, served on whole wheat bread and featuring baked sweet potato, a cashew aioli, pesto arugula, and caramelized onions. It's vegan and super tasty.

Naomi drew her inspiration for baking when she graduated from college and shipped out to Anchorage, Alaska, where she landed a job at the Fire Island Rustic Bake Shop. She took her knowledge, passion, and inspiration for baking that she nurtured in Alaska and brought it to her own shop in Coral Gables.

MADRUGA BAKERY DARK CHOCOLATE RYE BROWNIES

½ cup (1 stick) unsalted butter, cubed

6 ounces bittersweet chocolate, chopped

1¼ cups cane sugar

3 large eggs

¼ cup unsweetened cocoa powder

½ teaspoon salt

½ cup whole rye flour

1. Preheat oven to 350 degrees. Line an 8-inch-square baking pan with aluminum foil. Grease the foil with butter or cooking spray.

2. Place the butter and chocolate into a heat-proof bowl. Simmer water in a pan that the bowl can sit on top of, but not sink into, in order to create a double boiler. The bottom of the bowl should not touch the water. Stir the chocolate and butter over the simmering water until the mixture is smooth. Remove from heat, and let cool slightly.

3. Whisk the sugar into the eggs until totally combined. Slowly pour the chocolate-and-butter mix into the eggs and sugar, mixing as you pour.

4. Combine the cocoa, flour, and salt, and whisk together.

5. Gently fold the dry ingredients into the wet mixture, until you have a smooth batter.

6. Pour the batter evenly into the pan. Bake until set, about 35 minutes.

MAKES 9 BROWNIES.

Maroosh

Maroosh is a Mediterranean restaurant serving Lebanese cuisine, and it's best known for its delicious lamb entrées, such as rack of lamb, lamb loin chops, and lamb medallions. The restaurant has a relaxed ambience with tapestries on the walls, dark red curtains dressing the windows, and a gilded bronze Moroccan chandelier in the shape of a star—perfect for Maroosh's belly-dancing performances on Friday evenings.

A favorite lunch spot for locals, Maroosh offers large and filling lunch portions. You can't go wrong with their flavorful chicken kebab, the crispy falafel sandwich, or the gyro shawarma plate, well seasoned and tender and served with steaming jasmine rice and noodles topped with sliced almonds. Maroosh also makes an incredible baba ghanoush with roasted eggplant and hummus that is thick and creamy.

Maroosh features Lebanese wines on its list that are a perfect pairing for the Mediterranean dishes. Their Lebanese rosé is light and crisp with sweet tones and goes well with virtually any meal on the menu.

The perfect ending to a Maroosh dinner is a cup of strong Turkish coffee served in an ornate golden cup with a golden spoon, coupled with a sweet, sticky, nutty piece of baklava for dessert.

HUMMUS

1 cup uncooked chickpeas/
garbanzo beans
(yields 1½ cups cooked
chickpeas)

4 tablespoons tahini paste

Juice of 1 lime

2 garlic cloves

½ teaspoon salt

2 tablespoons plain Greek
yogurt or soy yogurt

Olive oil

Dash of sumac or paprika
for garnish

1. Soak the chickpeas overnight in plenty of water (water needs to be at least double the volume of chickpeas).

2. When ready, drain the chickpeas and place them in a medium-sized heavy cooking pot. Cover with plenty of water and boil for 1-2 hours.

3. Once fully cooked, transfer chickpeas immediately to a large colander over the sink. Run cold water while rubbing the chickpeas by the handful to remove the skins.

4. Place tahini, lemon juice, and garlic cloves in a food processor. Pulse for a few seconds to combine.

5. Add the cooked chickpeas, salt, and yogurt to the food processor. Purée until you achieve a smooth and creamy hummus dip.

6. Serve at room temperature or cooler, topped with olive oil and a dash of sumac or paprika. Use veggies and warm pita bread for dipping.

Mikuna

Mikuna, the latest Peruvian restaurant to open in Coral Gables, promises to be a welcome addition to the city's Peruvian culinary scene.

Mikuna is located in downtown Coral Gables on a quiet street north of Alhambra Plaza. The décor follows the traditional Peruvian look of dark wood with white walls. Although the restaurant is small, it's a fancy affair with white tablecloths.

Mikuna offers a lunch menu with bestsellers including lomo saltado, ceviche samplers, papa a la Huancaína, and causas. Health-conscious diners will find plenty to get excited about, with Mikuna's vegetarian dishes: mushroom ceviche, quinoa veggie chaufa (wok-fried quinoa with vegetables), innovative salads, and more.

You can't visit a Peruvian restaurant without having some ceviche, and Mikuna is no exception. The ceviche sampler features three types: rocoto red pepper ceviche, traditional Peruvian ceviche, and white ceviche with vegetables and seafood.

For desserts, go for the classic Peruvian offerings. The chocolate cake with dulce de leche is sweet and delicious, and the warm tres leches dessert will win a permanent place in your culinary heart.

MIKUNA LOMO SALTADO

2 tablespoons cooking oil

1½ pounds beef tenderloin, cut in ¼-inch strips.

1 red onion, cut in wedges

2 tomatoes, cut in wedges

1 red bell pepper, julienne cut

½ cup chopped fresh cilantro

⅓ cup low-sodium soy sauce

2 tablespoons red wine vinegar

3 tablespoons aji amarillo paste

salt, pepper, garlic, to taste

1. Heat the oil in a skillet on high heat, season the beef tenderloin strips with salt and pepper. Add beef to skillet until brown on both sides, then set aside.

2. In the same skillet, add the onion, red bell pepper, and garlic, and stir until softened. Add the soy sauce, aji amarillo paste, red vinegar, stir, and mix well. Add the tomatoes and the cooked beef strips. Just before serving, add the fresh cilantro.

3. Serve with rice and french fries.

SERVES 4.

MesaMar Seafood Table

MesaMar is a seafood fusion restaurant serving high-quality, fresh seafood innovatively prepared with Asian influences and Latin flavors and sauces in a lovely downtown Coral Gables setting. You'll find the creative combinations of seasonings, the upscale, elegant setting, and the jazz music playing lightly in the background to be mesmerizing.

The restaurant's interior features a library with backlit shelves full of books and maritime objects, giving the space a sophisticated look and feel. The main dining area contains tables adorned with white linens, and the room is illuminated by chandeliers made of sea-glass bottles.

Start your meal with perfectly cooked sea scallops or the savory tuna tartare. For an entrée, try MesaMar's famous Hog Snapper—half fried, half grilled, and paired with fried rice and tostones with garlic butter. The snapper is served upright on the plate in a dramatic presentation. The Seafood Paella and Parrillada de Mar (a plate with mussels, fish, prawns, lobster, and calamari) are also favorites with locals.

Finish off your MesaMar experience with a café bombon, espresso with condensed milk, paired with one of their delicious house-made desserts like the passion fruit-mousse or the almond praline.

Miss Saigon Bistro

Miss Saigon serves delicious, authentic Vietnamese cuisine. As you enter. you are greeted with Vietnamese music and servers dressed in traditional, flowing Vietnamese garb. The restaurant is decorated with bamboo panels and plants throughout, giving the place a cozy atmosphere. As soon as you sit down, hot towels are proffered to freshen up your hands and get you ready to enjoy your meal.

Miss Saigon's menu is based on chef/owner Mrs. Thi's recipes from her home. She personally created the menu, with additions from her children as they developed new recipes. Rick, one of her younger sons, came up with the restaurant's bestselling dish, the Miss Saigon, a steamed-rice noodle bowl filled with spring rolls and chicken. (Chef David recommends you ask for the spring rolls on the side so that they stay crispy until you are ready to eat them.)

For those looking for vegan options, try the watercress with seitan. It's a delicious combination of lightly stir-fried seitan (flavored wheat gluten) and crisp, fresh watercress. Other dishes to try include the Pho Soup and the spring roll appetizers. In terms of desserts, David recommends the chocolate and carrot cakes, which are baked at home by his wife, Lisa.

Morelia Gourmet Paletas

Morelia Gourmet Paletas brings a sweet note to the Miracle Mile. This purveyor of fortified, artisanal popsicles has quickly become a favorite for locals looking for a different twist on a cool treat.

Morelia, the popsicle shop's adorable sugar skull logo, greets you upon entering. The top shelf of the shop's interior is stocked with custom coolers featuring Morelia's likeness. The shop is bright with orange walls and giant photos of paletas on the walls. There are wooden tables to sit and enjoy your frozen treats with friends and family.

Pick your paleta from the shop's beautiful display cases. Morelia Paletas are as colorful as they are delicious. Each popsicle is made with fresh and natural ingredients. They offer a variety of 16 flavors, making it really hard to pick just one. Morelia Paletas offers many fruit and water-based options for vegan and dairy-free customers. For those who love rich, creamy desserts, they have an amazing selection of popsicles filled with condensed milk, Nutella, chantilly cream, and more.

Every paleta may also be garnished with flairs of white chocolate or milk chocolate dipping sauce and outfitted with six different toppings. This place is ideal for a dessert stop or a midday snack.

CHANTILLY
ULCE DE LECHE
EESECAKE
COOKIES 'N CREAM
PISTACHIO
YOGURT & BERRIES
CHOCOLATE
STRAWBERR
LIME & GING

S'MORES PALETAS

1 jar marshmallow cream or fluff

6 graham crackers

Metal spatula

4 chocolate popsicles

Food torch

1. Gently grind the graham crackers until they are almost a fine powder. Spread them on a clean plate or tray.

2. Using the metal spatula, evenly spread the marshmallow cream/fluff on the popsicles.

3. Use the food torch to slightly brown the marshmallow cream/fluff.

4. Place the popsicles on top of the graham cracker powder and press lightly, covering both sides.

SERVES 4.

My Ceviche

The first thing you notice when you walk into My Ceviche is the scent of freshly chopped cilantro. The restaurant's gorgeous interior features bright colors, natural wooden panels on the walls, giant modern pendant lamps, and a massive mural with their adorable shrimp logo wearing a chef's hat. The colorful industrial look of the seating area complements the white, subway-tiled kitchen with its bright blue ceiling made of corrugated metal.

Ordering at My Ceviche is quite a pleasant experience. As you browse the menu options, enjoy the upbeat reggae music that's piped into the eatery. Once you've decided whether you want tacos, a burrito, or a ceviche salad bowl, build your meal by surveying the ingredient stations, set up cafeteria-style. First you choose from a selection of different wraps. At the protein station, you can pick from wild-caught fish, shrimp, octopus, or free-range chicken. Then it's time to select from an array of tasty toppings, including cilantro, queso fresco, guacamole, mango, and many more. You then pay up, and you're free to feast. Don't forget to stop by the salsitas station. Your fish taco is not complete until you've added one of their signature salsas and a twist of lime.

CRISPY RED SNAPPER BURRITOS

COCONUT-JASMINE RICE

- 1½ cups jasmine rice
- 1½ cups water
- 1½ cups coconut milk
- 1½ white onions, diced
- 3 teaspoons sugar
- 3 teaspoons kosher salt
- 3 tablespoons canola oil
- 3 garlic cloves, chopped

PICKLED ONIONS

- 2 red onions, thinly sliced
- 2½ cups white vinegar
- 1¾ cups water
- 2 teaspoons sugar
- 2 tablespoons kosher salt
- 2 garlic cloves
- 1 jalapeño pepper, sliced

FILLING

- 6 12-inch flour tortillas
- 1½ cups grated queso fresco
- 2 Hass avocados, sliced
- 2 cups charred corn kernels
- 1 cup cilantro sprigs
- 1 cup radishes, sliced
- 1 cup pickled red onions

CRISPY RED SNAPPER

- 2 2-pound whole red snapper fillets, skin on
- 2 cups Wondra flour
- 1 quart cooking oil

COCONUT-JASMINE RICE

In a small pot over medium-high heat, add the oil then sweat the onions and garlic. Add the rice, salt, sugar, and the remaining liquid. Let simmer uncovered for about 10 minutes, until the liquid has evaporated. Cover the pot with a lid, and turn the heat to low. Let stand for about 10 to 12 minutes until the rice is completely tender.

PICKLED ONIONS

In a small pot, add the vinegar, water, salt, sugar, jalapeño, and garlic. Bring to a boil, then turn off the heat. Add the red onions, cover, and let stand until the mixture has cooled down.

CRISPY RED SNAPPER

Dust the red snapper fillets evenly on all sides with Wondra flour. Fry in oil at 375 degrees for about 4-5 minutes, until golden and crispy. Season with sea salt.

CILANTRO-GINGER MAYO

- 1½ cups mayonnaise
- 1 bunch cilantro, roughly chopped
- 2 jalapeño peppers, seeded and charred on grill
- 1 garlic clove
- ½ cup Key lime juice, freshly squeezed
- 1 tablespoon ginger, chopped
- 2 teaspoons kosher salt

Add all the ingredients into a blender, and mix on medium-high speed until all ingredients have come together.

TO ASSEMBLE

Grill the tortillas lightly on one side. Add ½ cup of rice per tortilla, then layer all the fillings evenly. Top with chunks of crispy red snapper. Roll by folding both sides inwards, about 2 inches over the filling. Roll the front flap forward, creating a roll. Slice in half. Serve with mayo on the side.

SERVES 6.

My Cupcake World

My Cupcake World recently opened in Coral Gables, offering beautifully decorated cupcakes and comfort foods. What started as a hobby evolved into a cupcake empire for Cupcake World owner and baker Iris Casanova. You can now find Cupcake World cupcakes at local farmer's markets, supermarkets, bakeries, and now at its very first brick-and-mortar Cupcake World store in the heart of Coral Gables.

The quaint yet lavish space boasts an explosion of pastel colors, including a turquoise typewriter and a pastel pink rotary wall-telephone. The walls are striped pink and white. The shelves are filled with pastel cake stands, and cupcake toppings include tubs of sprinkles in a rainbow of colors. The space is the epitome of cute. This is the perfect place to have a children's party with cookie and cupcake-decorating activities or to enjoy a modern-kawaii high tea with a treat cart of sweets.

The cupcakes are moist, delicious, and not overly sweet. Before indulging, try their famous tomato bisque soup with a grilled cheese sandwich. Also recommended are the gourmet artisanal empanadas named after fascinating women, such as Eleanor Roosevelt, Audrey Hepburn, Coco Chanel, Marie Curie, Georgia O'Keefe, and Celia Cruz.

APPLE OF MY EYE GRILLED CHEESE

2 pieces thick-sliced toast, well buttered

¼ thinly sliced green apple

½ teaspoon brown sugar

½ teaspoon ground cinnamon

1 teaspoon Crafted House-brand cinnamon butter

2 slices Brie cheese

Slivered almonds

1. Place the slices of thick, buttered bread on a preheated pan over medium heat until light brown.

2. Remove from pan and spread cinnamon butter on each side of the toast.

3. Place sliced Brie cheese in the pan; it will start to melt very quickly. Immediately add the thin apple slices, brown sugar, and ground cinnamon.

4. Use a spatula to transfer the cheese mixture onto the bottom slice of toast. Return the bottom slice to the pan.

5. Sprinkle on a few slivered almonds. Place the top bread slice and continue to turn the sandwich until perfectly toasted.

SERVES 1.

Ms. Cheezious

Ms. Cheezious of Coral Gables is a brick-and-mortar outpost of the grilled cheese food truck that rolled on to the streets of Miami in 2010. The humble cheese truck was an instant hit, serving everyone's favorite comfort food: grilled cheese sandwiches.

Ms. Cheezious is a fast-causal restaurant where you are meant to feel comfortable. They have a large selection of board games to play while you wait for your food. The space features beautiful dark-wood floors and a neon sign of their mascot, Ms. Cheezious, a pin-up maven sitting on a grilled cheese sandwich.

The menu offers delicious, somewhat decadent sandwiches, sides, and over-the-top milkshakes. Some of their bestselling menu items include the Croqueta Monsieur, a nod to local flavors with melted cheese over ham and croquetas sandwiched between golden toast; the S'mores Melt, a warm Nutella sandwich with graham cracker chunks and gooey melted marshmallows; and the Pastelito Milkshake, a vanilla-and-guava concoction topped with whipped cream and a fresh guava pastelito.

You may also get creative with the "Build Your Own Grilled Cheese," where you pick from an array of ingredients to create your own custom grilled cheese sandwich.

Pascal's On Ponce

Pascal Oudin, chef and owner of award-winning French restaurant Pascal's on Ponce, started cooking professionally at the age of 13. Over his long and varied career, he has worked with French culinary masters like Roger Verge, Joseph Rostang, Gaston Lenotre, and Jean-Louis Palladin.

In 2000, Oudin realized a lifelong dream and opened Pascal's on Ponce, an intimate 55-seat French restaurant with sublime contemporary French cuisine, featuring the freshest local ingredients and utilizing the classical French cooking techniques he learned from the masters.

Pascal's is the perfect restaurant for a special night out to experience traditional French fare. You may sample flavorful, nicely presented French dishes like duck terrine, cheese soufflé, escargot, twice-baked gruyere, and duck confit.

Start your Pascal's dinner with the famous lobster bisque and the haricot vert salad. Enjoy some wine or a cocktail with your entrée, and be sure to save room for dessert. Pascal's is known for its bittersweet chocolate soufflé with warm chocolate ganache, its crème brûlée with a crunchy top, and its baked Alaska served with strawberry and vanilla ice cream and a Grand Marnier meringue.

Ortanique on the Mile

Chef Cindy Hutson is the owner and chef of Ortanique on The Mile, a landmark on Miracle Mile for the past two decades. Ortanique serves what Cindy calls "Cuisine of the Sun"— diverse, seasonally driven, flavorful Caribbean dishes. It's fitting that Hutson coined the phrase to describe her cooking style, as she is as unique as her cooking.

Walking through the doors at Ortanique feels like stepping out of Miami and onto a plantation porch in Jamaica. There are string lights and draped colorful textiles separating different sections of the dining room into private cabana-like dining areas.

Cindy suggests starting with Red Stripe beer-steamed Mediterranean mussels or clams served in a spicy Red Stripe broth with shallots, scotch bonnet pepper, tomatoes, and Jamaican thyme.

For your main entrée, the certified Angus beef tenderloin is rich in flavor after being slowly roasted in a 72-hour sauce. It's a great dish for meat lovers, and it's served with truffle manchego mashed potatoes, sautéed asparagus, and a shiitake mushroom demi-glace.

Finish your meal on a sweet and cool note with warm guava bread pudding accompanied by a generous scoop of ice cream.

JERK CHICKEN PENNE PASTA

4 pounds marinated boneless, skinless chicken breast

1½ cups julienne shiitake mushrooms

½ cup sun-dried tomatoes

1 bunch chopped scallions

¼ cup fresh basil chiffonade

3 tablespoons salted butter

2 cups heavy cream

1 tablespoon Better Than Bouillon, chicken flavor

2 pounds cooked penne pasta

Salt and pepper, to taste

MARINADE FOR CHICKEN

½ cup olive oil

¼ cup teriyaki sauce

2 tablespoons prepared Caribbean jerk paste (or powder)

2 cloves fresh minced garlic

½ cup minced yellow onion

1. Place the butter in a large skillet over medium-high heat.

2. Sauté the chicken until halfway cooked. Add the mushrooms, tomatoes, heavy cream, and chicken bouillon.

3. Sauté for about 3 minutes until cream has thickened, then toss in the scallions and basil.

4. Cook the pasta as recommended and toss with the sauce.

SERVES 8.

MARINADE FOR CHICKEN

1. Mix all the ingredients in a stainless steel bowl with a whisk.

2. Julienne-cut the boneless breast into bite-sized strips.

3. Place the chicken in the marinade and let stand for at least an hour.

4. Pour off the excess marinade and prepare as described in the recipe above.

Palme d'Or

Located in the historic Biltmore Hotel, Palme d'Or is the pinnacle of fine dining in Coral Gables. White-gloved servers in tuxedos transport you through a six- or 11-course tasting menu that pays homage to the cuisine of France with some modern twists.

The Palme's traditional décor of carved crown molding, sparkling chandeliers, and mirrored columns take guests back to a time of Old World charm. The tables sport crisp, white linens and meticulously polished silverware and glassware. Sit outside at a table by the pool for a romantic atmosphere that is unparalleled.

With no à la carte ordering, surrender yourself to a truly sophisticated, multicourse French meal prepared by Michelin-starred Chef Gregory Pugin. "I like to prepare classic French dishes and add a slight twist of modernity to them. I am looking for that perfect balance and to give each guest a unique and amazing meal."

The tasting menus typically start with an amuse-bouche and end with a dessert selection. The cheese cart is loaded with amazing offerings from around the world. Each course is presented with a detailed explanation and a complementary wine pairing. There is no better dining experience in Coral Gables than a meal at the Palme d'Or.

LES MADELEINES

½ cup flour

1 tablespoon baking powder

Zest of 2 lemons

3 eggs

¼ pound (1 stick) butter, melted

1½ cups sugar

2 tablespoons Acacia honey

1. Preheat the oven to 350 degrees.

2. Whisk the eggs, then add the sugar and lemon zest.

3. Stir in the melted butter and honey.

4. Mix with the flour and baking powder until a homogenous mixture is obtained.

5. Refrigerate for 24 to 48 hours.

6. Pour the mixture into madeleine molds. Bake for about 7 minutes until a caramel color is achieved.

7. Remove from oven and cool down on a wire rack.

SERVES 4.

Pincho Factory

South Florida's most popular burger place, Pincho Factory takes an American staple and incorporates local flavors to create unique and delicious combinations. This casual and hip burger shop won Best Burger at Burgerlicious, Coral Gables's annual burger festival. If you're looking for lots of flavor and all things burger, Pincho Factory is the perfect spot.

The restaurant has modern-meets-industrial décor with exposed A/C ducts, natural wood, and chalkboard walls decorated with stylish, hand-lettered artwork. Order at the counter, and your food is delivered to your table.

The original Pincho Factory Burger is a local favorite, served with lettuce, tomato, pink sauce, matchstick potato chips, cheese, and a perfectly cooked patty. For those looking for more exotic flavors, try the Toston Burger—a patty and melted cheese sandwiched between two tostones (crispy, fried plaintains). The Fritanga Burger brings a taste of Nicaragua by adding a thick piece of fried white cheese, coleslaw, and crema.

Pincho Factory has garnered a reputation for their burgers, but they have a balanced and varied menu that includes pinchos (skewers), hot dogs, wraps, rice bowls, and salads.

3 pretzel buns

1 pound beef blend (short rib, brisket, chuck)

   Pimento goat cheese (recipe below)

   Beer onions (recipe below)

   Whole-grain mustard

   Kosher salt

PIMENTO GOAT CHEESE

8 ounces goat cheese

1 tablespoon paprika

½ tablespoon granulated garlic

¼ tablespoon kosher salt

¼ tablespoon black pepper

BEER ONIONS

2 medium red onions, cut into ½-inch-thick, half-moon slices

4 ounces Sam Adams Octoberfest beer

6 tablespoons brown sugar

1 tablespoon kosher salt

½ tablespoon black pepper

3 tablespoons olive oil

BEER ONIONS

1. In a medium sauté pan, heat the olive oil over medium-high heat.

2. Add the onions and cook until soft and translucent, about 3 minutes.

3. Add the brown sugar, salt, and pepper and cook until the sugar has dissolved and caramelized.

4. Add the onions and reduce the heat to medium. Allow to simmer until the beer has reduced, about 10 minutes.

FOR THE BURGER

1. Form three ⅓-pound patties with the beef blend. Season with salt (or seasoning of your choice), and grill at 350-400 degrees to desired doneness.

2. Slice the pretzel buns in half and toast on the grill for about 2 minutes on each side.

3. Top each burger with a tablespoon each of pimento cheese and beer onions.

4. Place the burger patty on the bottom slice of the pretzel bun. Smear 1 teaspoon of whole-grain mustard on the top slice of the pretzel bun and top off the patty.

SERVES 3.

Plomo Tequila & Taco Bar

Visit Plomo Tequila & Taco Bar for a trendy, artsy atmosphere in which to dine and imbibe. This Mexican-inspired eatery offers good food and a truly cool space.

The ceiling of this beautiful restaurant is covered with green vines intertwined within thick, rustic, wooden beams and string lights, giving the place an earthy feel. The bar top is a collage of different ceramic tile designs. Most of the seating is composed of high-top tables and bright metal stools with a weathered finish. The outside patio is decorated with cactus plants, a ceramic clay-tiled floor, and string lights, with giant murals on the walls reminiscent of lowbrow tattoo artwork.

Start off with guacamole and chips. The guacamole is made with lime, cilantro, sunflower seeds, and chopped tomato. Tacos make up much of the rest of the menu. Try the bestselling El Guero, made with beer-battered shrimp, creamy chipotle aioli, and pickled onions, all folded into a soft flour tortilla.

Also check out Plomo for their drinks, including strong, handcrafted margaritas, sangrias, and micheladas. One of the top dishes at Plomo's brunch is their eggs Benedict, served with chorizo, sope (fried corn tortillas), and Hollandaise sauce.

MOJO PORK TOSTONES WITH CURTIDO

MARINADE

- ¾ cup extra virgin olive oil
- 1 cup cilantro / coriander, lightly packed
- 1 tablespoon orange zest
- ¾ cup orange juice, fresh
- ½ cup lime juice
- ¼ cup mint leaves, lightly packed
- 8 garlic cloves
- 1 tablespoon fresh oregano leaves, packed (or ½ tablespoon dried oregano)
- 2 teaspoons ground cumin
- 1 teaspoon salt
- 1 teaspoon black pepper

PORK

- 4 pounds pork shoulder, skinless and boneless
- Mojo sauce (see below)
- 2 tablespoons lime juice
- ¼ cup orange juice
- Salt and pepper

MOJO SAUCE

- 2 tablespoons lime juice
- ¼ cup orange juice
- Salt and pepper

1. Combine the marinade ingredients in a food processor and blend until the herbs and garlic are finely chopped.

2. Place in a large Ziplock bag with the pork. Place in the refrigerator overnight.

3. Remove the pork from the marinade bag and bring to room temperature. Reserve the marinade.

4. Preheat the oven to 325 degrees. Place the pork on a rack in a roasting dish. Cover with a lid or double layer of foil, slightly tented so it is not pressed tightly against the pork.

5. Place in the oven and bake for 2 hours and 30 minutes. Then remove the foil and return to the oven for a further 30 minutes to brown.

6. Remove from the oven and place on a plate, loosely covered with foil. Rest for 20 minutes before serving with the Mojo Sauce on the side.

MOJO SAUCE

Place the reserved marinade, Mojo sauce ingredients, and 2 tablespoons of the roasting pan drippings into a small saucepan. Bring to boil and add salt and pepper to taste. Pour the Mojo sauce over the sliced pork.

SERVES 8.

PokéBao

PokéBao brings a fresh and unique twist to Hawaiian-style poké bowls and Asian-inspired bao buns. Chef Daniel Bouza has crafted a menu with a fusion that includes local flavors. Every single item on the menu is unique and delicious.

The restaurant's vibrant and modern use of reclaimed wood radiates a casual, cool atmosphere. The half-booths are made of recycled, painted, wooden pallets with mason jar vases on each table. The surf competitions shown on the TVs and reggae thumping through the speakers give the feeling of being at the beach.

Order one of PokéBao's tasty poké bowls, buns, and bites. Chef's Signature Poké Bowls include DB's Spicy Ahi Tuna Poké—furikake rice, yellow fin, masago, fuego mayo, and green onion; and Wasabi-furikake Salmon—furikake rice, sake-cured salmon, Maui onion, avocado, edamame, wasabi-cilantro aioli, and ikura. Chef's Signature Buns feature savory options ranging from DB's Sweet and Spicy Short Rib Bun to Crispy Chicken Vaca Frita.

Imported Japanese beer, local brews, and Hawaii-based Kona Brewing Company varieties are available as well as wine and the chef's personal selection of premium sakes.

AHI-SAKE MEDLEY

Mixed greens

2 fluid ounces + 1 tablespoon carrot ginger dressing

2 ounces fresh yellow tuna

2 ounces salmon

¼ cup ponzu sauce

3 cherry tomatoes, halved

¼ cup edamame, cooked, cooled, shelled

salt to taste

Black sesame seeds

White sesame seeds

Red onion slices for garnish

1. Toss the mixed greens with the carrot ginger dressing. Add salt to taste.

2. Toss the tuna, salmon, edamame, and cherry tomatoes with 1 tablespoon of carrot ginger dressing and ponzu.

3. Place the fish on top of the salad mixture. Top with white and black sesame seeds.

4. Garnish with red onions.

SERVES 2.

CHEF DANIEL BOUZA

In 2009, Miami-born and -raised Daniel Bouza decided to make a change from engineering to pursue his passion, departing for culinary school in New York City. He attended the Institute of Culinary Education and landed an externship at the Gotham Bar & Grill. He eventually opened BLT Bar & Grill in the Financial District, then opened four more restaurants in three years.

On a trip to Hawaii, Bouza was lured to stay by the beauty and magic of the island of Lana'i. During his time cooking at Nobu Lana'i, he developed a passion for Hawaiian-styled and Asian-inspired foods such as poké bowls and bao buns. Daniel found his way back to Miami, where he combined poké bowls and bao buns and offered them in a fast-casual restaurant environment. PokéBao is Chef Bouza's realized dream of combining these two cherished dishes.

Pummarola Pizzeria

The story of Pummarola starts in 1968 with Italian family matriarch Rosa Donna Rummo zooming through the streets of Naples in a bright-red Fiat 500. The shiny, chubby little car resembled a tomato on wheels, earning its name "Pummarola" (Neapolitan for "tomato"). Back then, the Fiat-driving "Nonna" owned a pizza and pasta restaurant lovingly named Pummarola.

Fast forward 45 years to 2013, when four of Rosa Donna's grandsons opened the Coral Gables Pummarola in honor of their grandmother's cooking. This reincarnation of Pummarola serves traditional Neapolitan Italian fast food and displays a replica of Nonna's adorable Fiat 500. All of the ingredients used at Pummarola are imported from Italy, including the flour, the tomatoes, and the olive oil. Equipped with a brick oven set at a blazing 900 degrees, the master pizzaiolos bake pizzas in a minute flat. So, if you are searching for an authentic Neapolitan Margherita pizza, this is the place to go.

For a fun experience, you can actually learn to make pizza with the master pizzaiolos at Pummarola. Every Saturday from 4 to 6 p.m., Pummarola offers a group pizza class where they teach you how to make pizza from scratch.

PUMMAROLA NEAPOLITAN PIZZA

16 ounces room-temperature water

Pinch of fresh beer yeast

2 tablespoons salt

2½ pounds flour

1 tablespoon olive oil

12 ounces tomato sauce

16 ounces shredded mozzarella cheese

1. Mix all the ingredients together in a large bowl into a big, soft, uniform, round ball of dough, approximately 15 minutes.

2. Cut the dough ball into two parts, and work each with your hands to make two separate balls.

3. Sprinkle a little olive oil on top of each dough ball. Cover them with plastic wrap and let rise for 12 hours.

4. Preheat the oven to 450 degrees.

5. Remove the plastic wrap, sprinkle some flour on a table or countertop, and using a rolling pin, roll out each dough ball into shapes big enough to fit a pizza pan.

6. Spread the tomato sauce and fresh mozzarella on each pizza, then put the pizzas in the preheated oven. Bake for 15 to 20 minutes until the crust turns golden brown.

7. Remove the pizzas from the oven, top with some fresh basil and a sprinkling of extra virgin olive oil, and cut into slices.

SERVES 4.

New and Notable on Giralda Plaza

Giralda Plaza, the "restaurant row" of Coral Gables, has experienced a recent surge of new restaurants on the venerable street. The pedestrian-only plaza is thrilled to have these new businesses join the City Beautiful's thriving downtown.

CLUTCH BURGER

Clutch Burger, offering a wide variety of wagyu beef burgers, opened on Giralda in 2018. With menu items ranging from the Volcano Burger and its signature charcoal bun to the Swolf Burger with pork belly, chorizo, white cheddar, onion rings, and sweet barbeque sauce, the company stays true to its motto, "Never Basic, Always Clutch."

MARA BASQUE CUISINE

Giralda Plaza gained an elegant addition with the arrival of Mara Basque Cuisine and Lounge. With a menu focused on specialties of the Basque region of Spain, including tapas, paellas and Lubina A La Sal, a unique dining experience is in store for all.

LORENZO PIZZA

Lorenzo Pizza brings a taste of Italy via Argentina, with authentic Argentinian-style pizza, panini, and wraps.

77 SPORT BAR

With wall-to-wall TVs and memorabilia from the renowned Barcelona Club Futbol, 77 Sport Bar is Giralda Plaza's go-to destination for great food and a lively atmosphere to watch every sporting event.

120 GIRALDA

Renovations are underway at 120 Giralda Plaza, Coral Gables's newest culinary destination, where the original façade is being revitalized to its original 1940s design. Coral Gables can look forward to the newest outpost of Coyo Taco and the first rooftop restaurant in Coral Gables, which will be helmed by Barley's Executive Chef Jorgie Ramos. New York City import Numero 28 joins the dynamic mix, with a wood-fired pizzeria, house-made pastas, and traditional Italian selections in a casual, contemporary atmosphere.

Raw Juce

This all-organic juice bar, part of a highly successful South Florida chain, offers cold-pressed juices, acai bowls, smoothies, salads, oatmeals, and other nutritious options for the health-conscious. Everything they serve is USDA-certified organic, fresh, and all the non-juice items are made in-house daily. Everything at Raw Juce is served raw, retaining the nutritional integrity of the entire product line.

Raw Juce's high ceilings create the look and feel of a large open space. The walls are covered in chalk paint, and the behind-the-bar menus are rendered in colorful hand lettering. Dark-brown leather chairs invite customers to linger inside. Outside, there are jacked-up café tables and chairs for those wishing to dine and sip alfresco when the weather is nice. Raw Juce is conveniently located next door to a popular yoga studio. The juice bar is the perfect place to grab some healthy refreshment after a session on your yoga mat.

All the juices bottled and in the display case are cold-pressed—the best method for getting the most out of fresh juice. Cold pressing ensures that vital enzymes, nutrients, and minerals stay intact. The acai bowls are colorful vessels of tasty nutrition and come highly recommended by the staff and many loyal customers.

OVERNIGHT OATS

1 quart Raw Juce Almond Milk

1¼ pounds Quick Oats

Garnishes

Mix in a bowl and let soak overnight refrigerated. In the morning, garnish with fresh fruit, coconut flakes, honey, or other garnishes of your choice.

SERVES 6.

Rice Mediterranean Kitchen

The latest build-your-bowl concept to arrive in Coral Gables, Rice Mediterranean Kitchen serves eastern Mediterranean cuisine with healthy options and nutritious ingredients. This is a popular lunch destination for locals looking for a fresh, quick meal in a beautiful setting.

The modern restaurant décor combines the textures of patterned tile walls, natural wood, exposed A/C ducts, string lights, and industrial metal dining chairs. They also have ample outside seating on Giralda Avenue, the pedestrian-only promenade in downtown Coral Gables.

Ordering at Rice Mediterranean Kitchen is easy. First, select the base of your bowl, choosing between basmati rice, brown rice, black lentils, or artisan super greens. Then select up to three dips or spreads from hummus, sriracha tomato hummus, honey nut feta, Greek yogurt sumac, charred carrot tahini, or eggplant harissa.

Next up is your protein selection: rustic falafel, roasted seasonal veggies, braised lamb, braised beef, harissa-roasted chicken, or slow-cooked chicken breast. Finally, add some toppings. Drizzle your choice of dressings and sauces over the top, and enjoy your bowl.

TURMERIC ROASTED VEGETABLES

12 ounces broccoli florets

12 ounces cauliflower florets

4–5 medium-sized organic carrots, peeled and cut into ¼-inch-thick slices

VEGETABLE DRESSING

The juice of 1 large lemon

½ teaspoon of tumeric powder

½ teaspoon salt

½ teaspoon black pepper

ROASTED GARLIC OIL

2 garlic cloves

¼ cup extra-virgin olive oil

MAKING THE DRESSING

1. Make the dressing by placing the garlic cloves and the olive oil in a small saucepan on low heat until the garlic cloves are very soft, about 7 to 9 minutes. (Make sure it's on low; otherwise the garlic may burn.) Allow to cool for a few minutes.

2. Stir in the fresh lemon juice, salt, turmeric powder, and cracked black pepper. Whisk together until well-combined, then slowly drizzle in the roasted garlic oil and continue to whisk/blend.

ROASTING THE VEGETABLES

1. Preheat oven to 350 degrees.

2. For the best consistency, roast the three vegetables in separate trays. This can be done in the same oven at the same temperature, paying close attention to the roasting times for each vegetable.

3. Whisk the dressing once again before use to ensure that all ingredients are distributed throughout and emulsified.

4. Gently mix the broccoli florets with half of the dressing, then arrange them in a single layer on a parchment-lined sheet pan. Roast for 20 minutes, then remove from oven and let cool.

5. Gently mix the cauliflower florets with ¼ of the dressing, then arrange them in a single layer on a parchment-lined sheet pan. Roast for 20 minutes, then remove from oven and let cool.

6. Gently mix the carrots with ¼ of the dressing, then arrange them in a single layer on a parchment-lined sheet pan. Roast for 35 minutes, then remove from the oven and let cool.

7. Toss all the vegetables together before serving.

SERVES 6.

Sacha's Café

Looking for a clean, well-lighted place to take a break from the workaday world of downtown Coral Gables? Give Sacha's Café a try. Located on the ground floor of a glass-and-steel office building and somewhat hidden down a walkway that opens onto Ponce de Leon Boulevard, this gem will help recharge your energy and spirits with its fine casual cuisine and superb coffees and teas.

Sacha's Cafés were founded by Hans Viertl and his wife, Sonia in the 1990s. Their mission is to offer high-quality breakfasts and lunches to local office workers seeking great food and good value. The restaurant's austere, bright-white-and-chrome décor is stylish and inviting. You may peruse many fresh-made salads and sandwiches in Sacha's lengthy, glass-encased deli counter or order from their extensive menu of breakfast and lunch sandwich offerings.

In addition to sandwiches and salads, Sacha's offers some fine hot dishes, including chicken cordon bleu, pan-seared salmon with a teriyaki glaze, stuffed crepes, and a fine chicken Milanese. The coffee offerings are some of the best in the city, including fresh brewed coffee, espresso, cappuccino, and various teas.

BLACK OLIVE TAPENADE SPREAD

½ pound kalamata olives, unpitted

2 anchovy filets

4 garlic cloves

2 tablespoons capers

1 lemon juice

5 tablespoons virgin olive oil

1. Wash the olives and remove pits.
2. Chop the garlic.
3. Add all the ingredients into a food processor.
4. Blend for 1-2 minutes. Should remain coarse.
5. Season with hot pepper if desired.

HUMMUS SPREAD

2 cups chick peas, drained

⅓ cup tahini paste

Juice of 2 lemons

Salt and cumin to taste

Garlic (optional)

1. Mix all ingredients in a food processor to make a smooth paste.
2. Add some lukewarm water.
3. Season with salt and cumin to taste.
4. Garnish in a bowl with extra virgin olive oil and cumin powder.

SERVES 4 AS A DIP OR SPREAD.

Salumeria 104

One of the newest additions to the Miracle Mile restaurant scene is Salumeria 104, the offspring of downtown Miami's highly successful Italian trattoria of the same name.

This cheerful, bustling spot has the look and feel of an intimate Italian delicatessen, yet it's a great place to grab a table or a stool and enjoy some fine food and drinks.

Salumi (Italian cured meats and cheeses) is the signature dish at this one-of-a-kind eatery. You may enjoy it with a glass of your favorite Italian wine or order it by the pound for takeout. (The Miami location has sold over 10,000 pounds of salume over the past 12 months.) Other popular dishes include the taglietelli Bolognese and the lasagna del Salumiere.

The restaurant's interior is bright and cheerful, with white-painted wood furniture and brick walls offset by several natural wood-colored tables. The front end of the space offers seating at tables and a long bar, while the deli space occupies the back, with slicers and scales for the salumi and well-stocked shelves displaying tempting selections of imported Italian gourmet foods.

Whether eating in or taking out, Salumeria 104 is a great new Italian spot to enjoy in the heart of town.

TAGLIATELLE BOLOGNESE

¾ pound ground veal

¾ pound ground pork

¾ pound ground beef

1 pint (3 cans) #10 peeled tomatoes

½ onion, finely chopped

2 celery stalks, finely chopped

2 carrots, finely chopped

¼ cup EVOO

½ bottle dry red cooking wine

1 teaspoon Kosher salt

1 teaspoon freshly ground black pepper

1 pound dry tagliatelle pasta

Freshly grated Parmigiano-Reggiano cheese

BOUQUET GARNISH

1 teaspoon black peppercorns

1 sprig rosemary

1 sprig thyme

1 sprig sage

1 bay leaf

1. Heat a heavy-bottomed pan. Add EVOO and all ground meat. Cook meat fully, continuously breaking it up with a potato masher or wooden spoon.

2. Once meat is cooked, add in all the chopped vegetables and cook for 10 minutes. Add the red wine and cook for 10 more minutes.

3. Add the tomatoes to the meat and stir well. Add the bouquet garnish and bring to a simmer. Cook for 1 1/2 hours.

4. When finished, add kosher salt and ground pepper.

5. Allow mix to rest for 5 minutes. Skim the fat off the top of the sauce using a ladle.

6. Break up all the remaining whole tomatoes with a wooden spoon or potato masher.

7. When you are ready to serve, bring a large pot of salted water to a boil, add the pasta and cook for 8 to 10 minutes or until tender yet firm. Drain the pasta well and toss with the Bolognese sauce.

8. Garnish with freshly grated Parmigiano-Reggiano cheese.

SERVES 4.

Shula's 347 Grill

Shula's 347 Grill, named after of Hall of Fame Miami Dolphins Coach Don Shula, is a steak house in the South of Coral Gables and home to one of the tastiest burgers in town. The upscale restaurant with classic décor is the place to go for business meetings or special occasions. Their superb service and romantic setting also make it a great destination for a romantic evening out.

The restaurant uses dim lighting to create the casual atmosphere of a traditional steakhouse with high-end flat screen TVs, leather seating, and dark wood. It's a popular destination for a drink after work or place to catch a game.

Start off your Shula's dining experience with fried calamari and the famous BBQ shrimp: 4 jumbo shrimp wrapped in bacon and covered with a caramelized barbecue sauce.

The filet mignon is the steak of choice, cooked to perfection with delicious seasonings. Shula's burger is also tops. The patty, made by blending short rib, brisket, and top sirloin, makes it super juicy. The fluffy bun is branded with the Shula's logo on top. Make sure to leave room for dessert: their banana chocolate chip bread pudding is a must!

Tinta y Café

In the northern reaches of Coral Gables, there's an adorable little Cuban café and coffee house tucked away on a quiet stretch of Ponce de Leon Boulevard. Tinta y Café is a bohemian throwback with a passionate local following—and with good reason.

Housed in a squat, 1960s-style ranch house structure set back from the street, the glass-fronted café beckons first with its walkup order window for busy locals looking to grab some coffee and a bite on their way to work. Step inside the café, and there's a riot of mismatched couches and tables, books displayed in square wooden frames in front of the windows, and an inviting counter with stools for solo sippers and diners.

The menu tends toward Cuban specialties, such as "El Tinta y Café," a sandwich loaded with pork, prosciutto, manchego, roasted red peppers, and carmelized onions. Another good sandwich choice is El Tropicana (aka the "Cuban Club"), which features turkey, sharp provolone, tomato, lettuce, and green olive tapenade. The espresso machine cranks out a wide variety of coffee drinks, and all juices are fresh-squeezed.

There are few places in the City Beautiful as warm and friendly as Tinta y Café, so seek this place out for an authentic bohemian coffeehouse experience.

Small Tea

Chef Agustin Silva Diaz and tea lover Daniel Benoudiz are the heart and soul behind Small Tea in Coral Gables. The tea shop, offering over 80 different types of tea and a small but delicious menu, has earned the loyalty of many locals.

The first time you visit Small Tea, take your time exploring the different types of loose teas on display in jars before making your decision. Even if you're not a tea drinker, there's a good chance you'll find a tea to fall in love with here. If you are already part of the growing tea movement, then this is the place for you.

Small Tea features one of the best examples of modern interior design in the city. It is sleek yet cozy. The walls and furniture are covered with wood panels and earthy tones. The back room features a curving wooden sculpture covering the walls and ceiling. Add to this the tasteful lighting and comforting acoustics, and you have the perfect haven to sit, relax, and enjoy a cup of fresh-brewed tea.

Small Tea is a truly beautiful space that makes you want to stay there and just be—with a nice cup of tea.

QUINOA EDAMAME POWER

16 ounces cooked tricolor quinoa

16 ounces cooked sweet corn

16 ounces cooked edamame

2 tablespoons diced red bell pepper

1 tablespoon diced green bell pepper

1 tablespoon diced red onion

3 tablespoons olive oil

2 tablespoons rice vinegar

Salt and pepper to taste

Mix all the ingredients together in a large bowl, and chill for at least an hour to allow the flavors to blend and come together.

SERVES 8-10.

Spring Chicken

Spring Chicken, the best place in Coral Gables for homemade chicken and biscuits, serves great food with Southern roots. They proudly make everything—from their secret recipe sauces to their fine fried chicken—from scratch in-house every day.

The restaurant has a rustic-meets-modern-barn feel with a big open space and upcycled wood covering the walls and ceiling. The back of the restaurant features a giant mural, and the indoor seating uses giant leather couches for booths. Outside seating is also available, including a long table nestled under a thicket of vines.

Spring Chicken recently started offering breakfast and brunch. Try the crispy chicken tender waffle sandwich with applewood-smoked bacon, griddled egg, and American cheese served on a savory cheddar cheese waffle. (They add bits of cheddar cheese to the waffle iron before pouring the batter to give the waffle added crunch.) For those with a sweet-tooth, try the freshly made, fluffy waffles served with berries, honey butter, and whipped cream.

Spring Chicken's lunch and dinner menu offers an embarrassment of riches when it comes to chicken. Choose from more than half a dozen types of chicken sandwiches, or opt for their famous lip-smacking Southern fried chicken in a variety of combinations.

SPICED WATERMELON

6½ pounds watermelon (after cutting)

1 ounce mint leaves, chopped

1 cup lemon juice

1. Take the watermelon and square off using a serrated bread knife. Trim off the outside layer and slice into 1-inch planks.

2. Cut the planks into 1-inch x 1-inch logs, then cut the logs into 1-inch cubes.

3. Add the chopped mint leaves and lemon juice and gently mix in a large bowl.

SERVES 6-8.

Sushi Maki

Sushi Maki offers great sushi that is delicious, made with responsibly sourced ingredients, and combines creative and tasty flavors. If you are looking for a high-quality, unpretentious sushi spot, this is the place.

Sushi Maki Coral Gables has a cool ambience that fits any occasion. Patrons dress anywhere from beach casual to button-down formal. There's a cozy patio with a great view of Ponce de Leon Boulevard, one of Coral Gables's busiest streets with lots of pedestrian traffic—great for people watching.

Sushi Maki offers a wide variety of nonsushi dishes from poke bowls and salads to Asian dishes like pad Thai, wok fried rice, red Thai curry, and teriyaki chicken. Their "cooked roll" section offers many selections for those trying sushi for the first time or those who don't want to eat raw fish. You'll find the traditional dragon roll—shrimp tempura, avocado, spicy mayo, and eel sauce—popular with locals, along with sushi boasting local flavors such as the cali ocho—krab, plantains, and mango guava ginger purée.

Sushi Maki is also known as the place to grab a bubble tea in the Gables. The popular sweet drink with tapioca bubbles is otherwise hard to find in the area.

SPICY TUNA SALAD

4 ounces fresh tuna, sushi-grade, in ½-inch cubes

½ Haas avocado, cubed into ½-inch pieces

1 teaspoon kimchee sauce

½ teaspoon sesame oil

1 pint field greens (romaine and spring mix)

2 ounces balsamic vinaigrette

¼ cucumber, thinly sliced

4 cherry tomatoes, halved

¼ teaspoon sesame seeds

2 ounces shredded carrots

1. Place cubed tuna and avocado into a small mixing bowl.

2. Add the kimchee sauce and sesame oil to another small bowl and gently mix.

3. In a medium mixing bowl, toss the salad greens with balsamic vinaigrette.

4. Place the greens onto a generously sized serving plate.

5. Top the greens with the tuna and avocado mix, and garnish with cucumbers, tomatoes, and shredded carrots.

6. Sprinkle with sesame seeds.

SERVES 1.

OWNER ABE NG

With integrity, ingenuity, and a true passion for better eating and living, Abe Ng was born to run restaurants. You might say it's in his genes. Abe's the son of immigrant restaurant operators. Today, he is the president, CEO, and CSO (Chief Sushi Officer) of Miami-based Sushi Maki and Canton Chinese Restaurants. In this role, he oversees the strategic development and management of all 18 locations owned and operated under the Sushi Maki and Canton brands and is a partner with Whole Foods Markets for sushi stations in South Florida region stores.

Taco Rico

Taco Rico is a laid-back restaurant near the University of Miami serving fresh, large, and tasty portions of Tex-Mex favorites like sizzling fajita platters and authentic Mexican fare, such as the Cochinita Pibil, all at affordable prices.

At this unassuming, cozy, and friendly family restaurant, you order at the counter. While you wait for your food, you'll receive a basket of crispy tortilla chips. Grab your preferred dipping sauce from the salsa bar, which offers pico de gallo, green salsa, limes, and three different red salsas.

Try their famous sizzling chicken fajitas served with flour tortillas, grilled onions and peppers, yellow rice, refried beans, cheese, and guacamole. Another popular menu item is the Wet Burrito, a massive burrito smothered in red salsa. Their lunch specials and platters of various combinations give diners virtually every option imaginable.

Taco Rico also has a variety of specials and deals throughout the week. Mondays are banner days for taco lovers on a budget. A buck will get you a taco. Students love this. Taco Rico also offers delivery for a quick, cheap, delicious meal for those too busy to stop in. You can't go wrong with Tex-Mex from Taco Rico, "the best Tex-Mex food North of the Border."

CORN AND BLACK BEAN DIP

12 ounces diced onion

1 diced red pepper

2 cans black beans

30 ounces canned or frozen corn

1 large bunch cilantro, chopped

Salt to taste

Cooking spray

1. Spray a pot with cooking spray and sauté the onion, pepper. Add in the corn after 3 minutes and continue stirring until warmed through.

2. Add in the beans, and cook through. Add the cilantro and continue stirring for a minute.

3. Transfer to a serving bowl, chill in the refrigerator for 30 minutes, then serve with tortilla chips.

MAKES APPROXIMATELY 1 QUART OF DIP. SERVE WITH TORTILLA CHIPS.

Talavera Cocina Mexicana

Talavera, the premiere Coral Gables destination for authentic Mexican fare, is located in the heart of the city. They offer an expansive menu inspired by a mix of traditional Mexican recipes and Mexico's contemporary cuisine.

Talavera's terracotta walls feature enormous, detailed murals, giving the restaurant a warm and welcoming ambience. The attention to detail can be seen in the authentic serveware dishes, glasses, shakers, and platters. Talavera, named after the most beautiful and refined handmade pottery in Mexico, serves their food in the white-and-blue clay dishes that inspired the restaurant's name.

Each meal begins with chips and salsa. Order one of their famous guacamoles for starters. All of their moles are made from scratch daily on the premises. Some of them use up to 36 fresh and authentic ingredients.

With their top tequila selections, Talavera is the go-to spot to grab a refreshing margarita. They offer interesting flavors like Pineapple Jalapeño, which tastes tart and refreshing with a spicy kick for a finish.

A few recommended dishes to try include the queso fundido, served bubbling hot and straight out of the oven; carne asada; and the enchiladas suizas.

ENCHILADAS SUIZAS

12 corn tortillas

2 pounds shredded chicken

Tomatillo-poblano cream sauce (recipe below)

1 pound shredded Oaxaca cheese

8 ounces Mexican cream

TOMATILLO-POBLANO CREAM SAUCE

2 pounds tomatillos, cut in half

1 serrano pepper

1 onion, chopped

3 cloves garlic

1 bunch cilantro

1 poblano pepper, chopped

1 cup zucchini, cubed

2 cups chicken stock

2 cups heavy cream

Salt to taste

You will need 4 personal baking dishes to serve this dish.

TOMATILLO-POBLANO CREAM SAUCE

1. Add all the ingredients in a large pot and bring to a boil.

2. Lower the heat and simmer for 15 to 20 minutes.

3. Let cool, then transfer to a blender and purée until smooth.

4. Mix well, season with salt, and reserve for the enchiladas.

ENCHILADAS

1. Preheat the oven to 375 degrees.

2. Heat the tortillas until pliable; place 2 ounces of shredded chicken on each tortilla, and roll to form an enchilada.

3. Sprinkle some salt inside each tortilla.

4. Place 3 enchiladas inside each of the baking dishes.

5. Pour the tomatillo-poblano cream sauce on top of the enchiladas and top each with 4 ounces of cheese.

6. Place the enchiladas in the preheated oven until the cheese is melted and golden; about 10 minutes.

7. Set four plates and carefully place the baking dishes on top of each plate.

8. Add the Mexican cream on top as a garnish.

SERVES 4.

The Bar

This Coral Gables classic was originally called the Hofbrau back in 1946, when it opened and was the first bar in Coral Gables. It began as a beer hall, and it has evolved through the years into the beer and classic cocktail venue we know today. The atmosphere of The Bar is dark and shadowy. Blue-hued walls reflect just enough of the dim light to create an atmospheric backdrop to enjoy a drink. The music from the jukebox is a loud mix of classic and contemporary rock.

With regard to the bar food–style menu, everything is made fresh in the establishment's small kitchen. Meat lovers should order the Barnyard Burger. The patty is made of brisket, ground beef, and smoked bacon that's mixed into the patty. The burger is augmented with more bacon and a fried egg on top. Black bean chicken chili comes on the side, but it can also be ladled onto your burger. All sandwiches are served with golden, crispy fries.

The Bar is open until 3 am, and their kitchen stays open until 2 am. So if you're hungry after a night on the town, stop in for a late night snack or meal.

BANG BANG SNAPPER

RICE PILAF

- 1 cup long grain white rice
- 2 teaspoons olive oil
- ¼ cup chopped onion
- ¼ cup chopped celery
- 2 cups chicken or vegetable stock
- 1 teaspoon salt
- ¼ teaspoon ground pepper
- ⅛ teaspoon cayenne
- ¼ cup chopped fresh parsley

BANG BANG SAUCE

- 1 tablespoon cooking oil
- 4 ounces Thai chile sauce
- 1 tablespoon fresh-squeezed lime juice
- 2 tablespoons sour cream
- 7 whole cherry tomatoes
- 2 ounces chopped cilantro

SNAPPER

- 2 8-ounce fresh red snapper fillets
- 2 cups panko
- 1 tablespoon Cajun spice
- ½ cup flour
- 2 eggs, beaten
- Salt
- Cooking oil

1. Heat the stock in a 2-quart saucepan over medium high heat. Stir in the salt, pepper, and cayenne.

2. While the stock is warming, heat the olive oil in a large skillet on medium high heat. Add the uncooked rice and stir for a couple of minutes until brown. Add the onions and celery and cook a few minutes longer, until the onions begin to soften.

3. Add the rice mixture to the heated stock, cover, and simmer until the rice is cooked, usually 15 to 25 minutes. Remove from heat and let sit covered for 10 minutes. Fluff with a fork and stir in the parsley. Cover and set aside.

4. Heat the cooking oil over medium high heat in a skillet. Add the cherry tomatoes until blasted, then add the Thai chili, lime juice, and sour cream.

5. Simmer for 3 minutes over medium heat, then set aside, adding the cilantro once it chills.

6. Preheat the oven to 350 degrees. Line a baking sheet with parchment paper and brush with cooking oil. Place the flour and beaten eggs in separate, shallow bowls. Combine the panko and Cajun spice in a third shallow bowl. Coat each fillet in flour, then thoroughly coat with the egg mixture. Then coat the fillets in panko, gently pressing it on to help it adhere, and set the fillets on the baking sheet.

7. Bake for 6 minutes, then carefully flip each fillet over. Bake 6 minutes more, or until flaky and just cooked through. Plate the fish and serve with the rice pilaf and Bang Bang sauce.

SERVES 2.

The Globe

The Globe, perhaps best known for its live jazz performances, is the perfect place to grab a drink or bite to eat after work. They have a generous happy hour on drinks Tuesday through Friday that stretches from noon until 8 pm, with a tempting 20 percent discount on appetizers. It's the perfect place for those who enjoy live music while sipping a drink and nibbling on tasty treats.

The Globe brings a touch of old-school restaurant charm to downtown Coral Gables. With décor reminiscent of 19th-century Parisian bars and restaurants, you'll find chandeliers, dark wood, and crown molding on the ceilings adorning a well-stocked bar that's the focal point of the space. The bar's top shelf is lined with globes of different sizes, a nod to the establishment's name.

The restaurant has a relaxed atmosphere with friendly service and a varied menu. You'll find everything from salads to burgers and quesadillas to hand-tossed pizzas. Some of their best-selling dishes include English ale fish and chips made with lightly battered, deep-fried cod and served with crispy french fries. The baked Cuban tostadas, baked brie, and chorizo with manchego cheese quesadillas are so tasty that customers typically devour them within seconds before ordering more.

BLACKENED ATLANTIC SALMON, LENTILS, AND RED QUINOA

4 6-ounce salmon filets

2 teaspooons extra virgin olive oil

4 lemon wheels

BLACKENED SEASONING
(Mix Together)

½ teaspoon kosher salt

½ teaspoon paprika

½ teaspoon garlic powder

½ teaspoon cayenne pepper

½ teaspoon thyme

½ teaspoon oregano

½ teaspoon sage

½ teaspoon onion salt

FOREST HONEY GLAZE
(Mix Together)

½ cup forest honey

Juice from ½ lemon

2 tablespoons balsamic reduction

1 teaspoon red pepper flakes

LENTILS AND RED QUINOA

2 cups lentils

2 cups red quinoa

SALMON, SEASONING, AND GLAZE

1. Place the blackened seasoning on a plate or flat surface. Coat both sides of the salmon filets with the seasoning.

2. In a large skillet over medium heat, add the olive oil. Add the salmon, skin side up. Cook salmon until golden, approximately 3 minutes. Flip over. Cook for a further 2 minutes.

3. Add the forest honey glaze mixture to the pan. Cook until the sauce is reduced by one-third.

LENTILS AND RED QUINOA

1. Add 6 cups of water to the lentils in a pot on the stovetop. Bring to a boil, cover tightly, and reduce heat and simmer until lentils are tender, approximately 15 to 20 minutes.

2. Rinse the quinoa in water. On the stovetop, boil 4 cups of water. Stir in the quinoa. Turn the heat down to low. Cover and simmer until liquid is absorbed. Use a fork to fluff and separate the grains.

Assembly: Mix the lentils and quinoa together. Place one quarter of the mixture on each plate, then top with salmon fillets. Pour some of the residual honey mixture from skillet onto the salmon. Add thin lemon wheels for garnish.

SERVES 4.

The Local Craft Food & Drink

If you enjoy lovingly made, creative comfort food, then head on over to The Local. Chef Phil Bryant has taken over this well-known gastropub and developed a menu firmly rooted in Southern cooking with a local twist. This is the place for fried chicken, craft beer, cheese boards, burgers, and charcuterie.

The Local has a relaxed pub feel with a gorgeous wooden bar, exposed-brick walls, and chalkboard menus that are updated constantly, as new beer and food options are rotated onto the menu. Even if you are a regular, you will always find something new and enticing to try.

Phil is always playing with innovative techniques and ingredients to come up with new, creative, delicious recipes. He has developed variations of Southern dishes by incorporating South Florida ingredients like mango, plantains, and yucca into his cooking.

If you are looking for a good burger, The Local has it. The patty is a bacon and brisket blend served with American cheese, pickled onion relish, and Mississippi Comeback Sauce. Brunch features innovative omelets and eggs benedict. With its quaint Spanish tile roof, The Local is easy to spot along crowded, busy Giralda Avenue.

PULLED HEN AND BUTTERMILK DUMPLINGS

1 stewing hen

2 Spanish onions

3 large carrots

4 stalks celery

3 bay leaves

1 bunch Italian parsley

PARMESAN BROTH

4 tablespoons olive oil

4 strips bacon, diced

8 parmesan rinds, chopped

4 cloves

2 bay leaves

1 quart heavy cream

DUMPLINGS

1 cup buttermilk

¼ pound of unsalted butter

½ teaspoon granulated garlic

½ teaspoon granulated onion

1¼ cup all-purpose flour

3 whole eggs

SOUP

4 tablespoons butter

24 dumplings

2 cups pulled hen meat

1 cup fresh corn kernels

1 Spanish onion, thinly sliced and browned

1 carrot, small dice

2 stalks celery, small dice

(Soup ingredients, cont.)

¼ teaspoon crushed red pepper

¼ teaspoon freshly ground black pepper

½ teaspoon kosher salt

2 tablespoons bourbon

1 cup reserved broth from cooking the hens

1 cup parmesan broth

¼ cup grated Parmesan cheese

HEN

In a large pot, place the hen and chopped ingredients. Cover with cold water. Bring to a boil, then turn down and simmer about 4 hours. Remove the chicken and allow to cool. Pull and mix white meat and dark meat evenly. Strain and reserve the broth.

PARMESAN BROTH

In a saucepot, heat the olive oil over medium heat. Add the bacon and brown. Add the cloves and lightly toast. Add the bay leaves, Parmesan rind, and heavy cream. Simmer and cook for 15 to 20 minutes. Strain and reserve.

DUMPLINGS

In a saucepot, add the buttermilk, butter, and spices. Bring to a boil and whisk in the flour. Cook over medium heat, stirring constantly, until a dough is formed. Remove from heat. Mix in the eggs one at a time. Wrap the egg/dough mixture loosely in greased baking paper and refrigerate.

Once the dough is cooled, cut into 4 equal portions. On a floured surface, roll the portions into logs, about 1 to 1 1/2 inches thick. Cut into 1-inch pieces and place on a floured tray. Refrigerate.

Bring a pot of salted water to a boil. Add the dough pieces, let them float to the surface, and cook for 1 minute. Remove from the water and drain well. Reserve.

SOUP

In a saucepot, melt the butter. Add the dumplings and cook until lightly browned. Add the hen, corn, cooked onions, celery, carrots, and crushed red pepper. Add the bourbon, and light on fire to cook out the alcohol. Add the chicken and Parmesan broths and bring to a simmer. Add the Parmesan cheese and cook until melted into the soup. Season to taste. Garnish with chopped chives.

MAKES 4 SERVINGS.

The Seven Dials

Seven Dials is a neighborhood English Pub located on the ground floor of an office building and owned by Coral Gables native Katie Sullivan and British expat Andrew Gilbert. They serve American fare with a British twist and always have craft beer from local breweries on tap. If you are looking for amazing fish and chips, this is the place to go.

The first thing you notice at Seven Dials is the whimsical wallpaper on the back wall. It features a collage of animals: a skunk having a drink, a lemur playing the accordion, a hedgehog, an otter with a fashionable fan, and many other creatures, all rendered with a vintage feel.

When you visit this English gastropub, order the fish and chips. Andy uses corvina as a local sustainable alternative to cod. He also uses a traditional beer batter that is crispy and fluffy outside, coating perfectly cooked fish within. It's served with fresh, hand-cut french fries.

For those seeking a classic British dish, give the bangers and mash a try. The sausages are from Proper Sausages butcher shop in Miami Shores, which is operated by another American/British couple. The British-style sausages are served with mashed potatoes, and both are smothered in onion gravy.

SMOKED SALMON KEDGEREE

8 ounces Scottish smoked salmon, cut into bite-size pieces

4 ounces firm white fish, cut into bite-size chunks

4 ounces medium shrimp, cleaned and deveined

4 eggs

1 teaspoon ground turmeric

2 teaspoons curry powder

2 cups uncooked basmati rice

2 tablespoons butter, divided

Juice of ½ lemon

Handful chopped cilantro

Salt and pepper to taste

1. Rinse the rice at least twice, using fresh water each time. Drain, then cook using 3 1/2 cups fresh water, 1 tablespoon of butter, and 1 teaspoon of salt.

2. Whisk all the eggs together with a pinch of salt in a bowl. Pour the eggs into a nonstick pan over low heat and cook until set, without stirring, for about 5 minutes. Remove from heat, cut into long ribbons, and set aside.

3. Heat 1 tablespoon of butter in a nonstick pan over high heat. Before the butter browns, add the white fish and shrimp.

4. Cook through, about 3 to 4 minutes, then add the cooked rice, smoked salmon, egg strips, spices, and half the cilantro.

5. Stir very gently with a wooden spoon to incorporate and heat everything through. Check for seasoning and adjust to taste. Top with a squeeze of lemon juice and the remainder of the cilantro.

SERVES 4.

Threefold Café

An Australian couple, Teresa and Nick Sharp, own Threefold Café, home to South Florida's most popular version of smashed avocado toast. This adorable café takes its coffee and breakfast seriously, and they serve up both all day.

Threefold has a warm and inviting atmosphere. The tables are made of wood with a rough finish, giving the restaurant a rustic look and feel. Bright yellow metallic chairs add a pop of color throughout the space. The cold drinks are served in mason jars, and swing-top glass bottles are set at each table and filled with water. There are tables with umbrellas outside on Giralda Avenue, Coral Gables's new, pedestrian-only promenade. It's a gorgeous location to enjoy a delicious Australian-style breakfast or brunch.

Threefold proudly serves coffee made from freshly roasted beans sourced locally from Panther Coffee. Their gourmet breakfast menu has ultimate brunch dishes like the aforementioned smashed avocado toast served on local bakery (Zak the Baker) bread. Also try the crushed beets or "Peas Please" toasts served in the same manner. You can add a poached egg on top of any of these exotic toast treats. Eggs, salads, sandwiches, and sweets round out the daily offerings at charming new oasis in the heart of Coral Gables.

CHEMEX POUR-OVER COFFEE

1 ounce of freshly roasted specialty coffee

16 ounces boiling water (plus a little more for washing the filter)

EQUIPMENT NEEDED:

Chemex coffee brewer

1 Chemex filter (paper)

Quality coffee grinder

Goose-neck water kettle

Timer

Scale

1. Weigh coffee out and grind to desired consistency.

2. Put the paper filter in the Chemex and gently pour hot water over the filter to wet and wash it, then discard the water.

3. Put the ground coffee into the damp filter, place the Chemex on top of the scale, and weigh it.

4. Start the timer and slowly pour boiling water over the coffee grounds, starting in the center then working out from the center to wet the coffee.

5. Pour 2 ounces over approximately 10 seconds.

6. Stop pouring and let the coffee "bloom."

7. At 45 seconds, continue slowly pouring boiling water in a circular motion over the wet coffee. Avoid pouring near the edges.

8. Continue this motion until the timer reads 2:30. The aim is to have the scales reading 17 ounces at this time.

9. Allow the water to continue running through the coffee until the stream stops and turns to a drip.

10. Discard the filter and coffee grounds.

SERVES 2.

Uvaggio

This little gem of a restaurant sitting right on Miracle Mile is a haven for wine lovers. Next time you are planning a special night out, call and make a reservation at Uvaggio. The food is fantastic, the wine list is carefully curated, and the atmosphere is perfect for an intimate culinary experience.

The floral accents decorating the walls give the illusion of a meadow of flowers hanging in the air. All the seating is at upscale high-top tables with comfortable stools. If you're a beer lover, there is a bar in the back of the restaurant where you may choose from the many beers on tap. The inside has only half a dozen tables, so be sure to make a reservation before arriving.

Uvaggio takes its wine very seriously. The entire front-of-house staff consists of trained sommeliers. Uvaggio offers between 30 and 40 wines by the glass every day, and it maintains a "cellar" of over 125 wines by the bottle. They also host special wine tastings every Saturday from 5 to 6 p.m., covering a new topic and focus each weekend. The menu consists of finger foods and tapas-sized plates carefully prepared to go with the many wine and beer selections.

BAHARAT-SPICED SHORT RIBS WITH CARROT PURÉE

5 pounds boneless short ribs

Extra virgin olive oil

Baharat spice rub

BAHARAT SPICE RUB

1 tablespoon black peppercorns

2 teaspoons coriander seeds

1 tablespoon cumin seeds

½ teaspoon whole clove

1 teaspoon ground cardamom

1 teaspoon ground cinnamon

1 teaspoon ground nutmeg

2 teaspoons dried lime zest

1 tablespoon smoked paprika

CARROT PURÉE

3 large carrots

1 orange (zest and juice)

½ cup extra virgin olive oil

Salt to taste

FENNEL RELISH

1 bulb fennel, diced

1 cup parsley, chopped

1 cup fennel fronds, chopped

2-3 tablespoons red wine vinegar

1 cup extra virgin olive oil

Salt to taste

PUFFED WILD RICE

½ cup wild rice

4 cups vegetable oil (for frying)

Salt to taste

BAHARAT SPICE RUB

Toast whole spices, then blend until you get a smooth mixture. Combine all the spices together.

SHORT RIB PREPARATION

Portion the short ribs into 6 to 8-ounce pieces. Rub with oil and cover in baharat spice mix. Put in vacuum seal bags with a small knob of butter and sous vide at 167 degrees for 24 hours. (Or bake in the oven at 300 degrees for 4 to 4½ hours until tender.)

CARROT PURÉE

Boil the carrots and orange zest for 10 to 15 minutes or until tender. Put in a blender, then add the orange juice and blend, adding oil until the mixture is emulsified. Add salt to taste.

FENNEL RELISH

Mix all ingredients to make a relish.

PUFFED WILD RICE

Bring the oil up too 400 degrees, and drop in the wild rice. Rice should puff up immediately. Remove with a slotted spoon on to paper towels. And salt to taste.

Once all the components are prepared, the carrot purée is plated first. Short ribs then go on top. Add the fennel relish and puffed rice to taste. Top with fennel fronds.

SERVES 6.

Veganaroma

For the taste of a home-cooked meal with a healthy twist, visit Veganaroma. All the ingredients at this Italian-inflected eatery are vegan, including their cheese and meatballs. The tiny storefront establishment is located on traffic-heavy 8th Street east of Ponce de Leon Boulevard. Drive around back where you'll find ample parking.

Veganaroma is a small and intimate affair. Two people run the restaurant at any given time, doing everything from greeting customers to waiting tables, cooking the meals, bringing the check, and inviting you back. Because every meal is made from scratch, be prepared to wait a bit for your custom-crafted vegan goodies.

Original owner Sabina Torrieri built a loyal clientele over more than a decade in business. Recently under new ownership, Veganaroma continues to specialize in vegetarian and vegan versions of classic Italian-American cuisine. The menu features a rotating hearty soup of the day, offering flavors like hearty, healthy minestrone or lentil. You'll find salads, ravioli, pizza, and pastas on the menu. The restaurant is particularly known for its raw lasagna and decadent yet healthy desserts.

Stop by this one-of-a-kind vegan Italian joint for a tasty, fresh meal, where the top priorities are keeping the food healthy and their customers satisfied.

VEGAN AND RAW LASAGNA DELL'AMORE

8 zucchinis, preferably organic, washed, and thinly sliced with mandolin

WALNUT "MEAT" SAUCE

½ cup chopped walnuts

½ cup sun-dried tomatoes

1 tablespoon tamari

1 teaspoon dried sage

2 tablespoons extra virgin olive oil

Pinch of Himalayan salt or sea salt

CASHEW CHEESE

1 cup chopped cashews

1 cup filtered water (less or more, as needed)

2 tablespoons nutritional yeast (optional)

2 tablespoons lemon juice

1 tablespoon apple cider vinegar

Pinch of Himalayan salt or sea salt

PESTO

¼ cup fresh basil (extra for garnish)

½ cup pine nuts or walnuts

½ cup extra virgin olive oil

1 tablespoon nutritional yeast (optional)

½ garlic clove

pinch of Himalayan salt or sea salt

TOMATO SAUCE

1 cup plum or Roma tomatoes

½ cup sun-dried tomatoes

⅔ cup dates

3 tablespoons extra virgin olive oil

1 teaspoon dried oregano

Pinch of Himalayan salt or sea salt

1. For the walnut "meat" sauce, grind all ingredients in a food processor, leaving the mixture slightly chunky.

2. For the cheese, process all ingredients together, adding a little water at a time, until a fluffy consistency is achieved.

3. For the basil pesto, pour all ingredients into a food processor or blender and mix until creamy.

4. For the tomato sauce, process all ingredients in a food processor or blender until smooth.

5. Make the lasagna by alternating a layer of zucchini, a layer of nut cheese, a layer of marinara sauce, a layer of walnut "meat," and repeat two more times, topping with sauce. (You can add a layer of spinach to make the lasagna a little taller).

6. Serve garnished with fresh basil and nut parmesan cheese.

SERVES 6.

Whip N Dip Ice Cream Shop

This family-run ice cream shop opened its doors in 1985 and won over locals with their unique frozen treats and delicious homemade hot fudge. They've been making light and fluffy ice cream for over 30 years. It's one of those local joints where you sit outside on a bench to enjoy your tasty treat and catch up with neighbors.

Located within a building painted in Miami Art Deco pink and green, Whip N Dip is an old-school, no-frills ice cream shop. All Whip N Dip products are made in-store with locally sourced ingredients. Buy it by the cone, the cup, or the cake. Fresh-baked cookies and frozen bananas are other popular items.

The flavor selection changes constantly with flavors like Guinness Vanilla, Red Velvet Chocolate, Banana Nut Chip, Birthday Cake, Bulldog Blitz (cotton candy ice cream, marshmallows and sprinkles), Chocolate Cheesecake, Cookie Combo, Heath Bar Brownie, Pineapple Sorbet, Snow-Capped Andes Chocolate, and many more.

With so many unique flavors, it's hard to pick just one. The Whip N Dip staff is friendly and quick to offer samples to try the different flavors. Stop by and take a break from the south Florida heat with a wonderfully sweet Whip N Dip treat.

BANANA BREAD

2–3 bananas, very ripe and peeled

⅓ cup melted butter

1 teaspoon baking soda

pinch of salt

¾ cup sugar

1 large egg, beaten

1½ cups all-purpose flour

Preheat the oven to 350 degrees.

Mix all the ingredients together in a large bowl.

Grease a 4 x 8 bread pan, or spray it with cooking oil.

Pour the mixture into the baking pan, and bake for 50 to 60 minutes, until a toothpick inserted in the center comes out clean.

Allow to cool.

SERVES 4.

Zucca

It's easy to fall hard for this gorgeous, relatively new Italian restaurant and high-end lounge. Located on the first floor of the historic Hotel St. Michel, the building's exterior is covered with ethereal vines that give the entire building a secret garden atmosphere. The elegant and seductive interior with beautiful bars features leather-tufted booths, rose-gold accents, and lively, European-inspired green walls.

Start your gourmet Italian meal with Arancini—crispy risotto balls stuffed with Bolognese ragu and mozzarella. At Zucca the dishes are rich and served in beautiful presentations. For your main dish, order one of the homemade authentic Italian pastas: Linguine alle Vongole, Gnocchi al Pomodorino, or Cacio e Pepe.

Zucca has also garnered praise for its extensive cocktail menu and its staff of expert mixologists. The signature Nonna's Mule is served with a refreshingly thin slice of watermelon. It's a hefty concoction that comes in a 12-inch-diameter lidded copper bowl. The drink is big enough to pass around and share with your companions.

Be sure to add Zucca's all-you-can-eat buffet to your list of Sunday brunches. You'll enjoy prosecco, pastries, pastas, and more. Don't leave without trying their famous Ferrero Brioche French Toast in all its chocolaty goodness.

FIORI DI ZUCCA RIPIENI DI RICOTTA E LIMONE
(Zucchini flowers stuffed with ricotta cheese and lemon)

6–8 zucchini flowers

1 cup fresh ricotta cheese

1 medium-sized zucchini

¼ cup Parmesan cheese

2 lemons

1 cup tempura flour

2 cups sparkling water

1 quart frying oil

Salt and pepper

1. Dice the zucchini in ¼-inch cubes.

2. In a mixing bowl, add the diced zucchini, ricotta cheese, and Parmesan cheese. Add a pinch of salt and pepper.

3. Add the juice of 1 lemon and the zest of 2 lemons.

4. Using a pastry bag, fill the zucchini flowers with the contents of the mixing bowl.

5. In a separate bowl, combine the tempura flour with the sparkling water to create a batter.

6. Heat the frying oil in a casserole pan to around 350 degrees.

7. Dip the zucchini flowers into the tempura batter and fry in the pan until golden brown.

SERVES 2.

Contact Information

Aragon 101
101 Aragon Avenue
(305) 443-7335

Aromas del Peru
1930 Ponce de Leon Boulevard
(305) 476-5885

Bangkok Bangkok II
157 Giralda Avenue
(305) 444-2397

Bellmont Spanish Restaurant
339 Miracle Mile
(786) 502-4684

Biltmore Culinary Academy
1200 Anastasia Avenue
(305) 913-3131

Bulla Gastrobar
2500 Ponce de Leon Boulevard
(305) 441-6107

Café at Books & Books
265 Aragon Avenue
(305) 448-9599

Caffe Abbracci
318 Aragon Avenue
(305) 441-0700

Caffe Vialetto
4019 South Le Jeune Road
(305) 446-5659

Chef Sucre Café
475 Biltmore Way, #104B
(305) 444-2025

Chocolate Fashion
248 Andalucia Avenue

(305) 461-3200

Christy's
3101 Ponce de Leon Boulevard
(305) 446-1400

Cibo Wine Bar
45 Miracle Mile
(305) 442-4925

Copper 29
206 Miracle Mile
(786) 580-4689

CraveClean Protein Bakery
3822 SW 8th Street
(786) 534-2144

Crema Gourmet
169 Miracle Mile
(786) 360-4026

Delicatessen Patagonia
244 Miracle Mile
(305) 640-8376

Divino Ceviche
160 Giralda Avenue
(786) 360-3775

Eating House
804 Ponce de Leon Boulevard
(305) 448-6524

Fontana Biltmore
1200 Anastasia Avenue
(305) 913-3189

Fratellino Ristorante
264 Miracle Mile
(786) 452-0068

Fritz and Franz Bierhaus
60 Merrick Way
(305) 774-1883

Gastronomicom
2151 Le Jeune Road, Suite 110
(786) 534-7325

Graziano's Restaurant
394 Giralda Avenue
(305) 774-3599

Graziano's Market
2301 Galiano Street
(305) 460-0001

Gusto Fino
271 Alhambra Circle
(305) 444-0504

House Kitchen and Bar
180 Aragon Avenue
(786) 482-5599

John Martin's Irish Pub
253 Miracle Mile
(305) 445-3777

Kao Sushi & Grill
127 Miracle Mile
(786) 864-1212

La Dorada
177 Giralda Avenue
(305) 446-2002

Lan Ramen-Ya
357 Alcazar Avenue
(305) 442-8600

Le Provençal
266 Miracle Mile

(305) 448-8984

LOUI
271 Miracle Mile
(786) 534-8888

Madruga Bakery
1430 South Dixie Highway,
Suite 117
(305) 262-6130

Maroosh
223 Valencia Avenue
(305) 476-9800

MesaMar
264 Giralda Avenue
(305) 640-8448

Mikuna
325 Alcazar Avenue
(786) 420-2910

Miss Saigon Bistro
148 Giralda Avenue
(305) 446-8006

Morelia Gourmet Paletas
76 Miracle Mile
(833) 423-7677

Ms. Cheezious
1915 Ponce de Leon Boulevard
(786) 518-3369

My Ceviche
232 Miracle Mile
(786) 409-7329

My Cupcake World
262 Andalucia Avenue
(305) 456-0950

Ortanique on the Mile
278 Miracle Mile
(305) 446-7710

Palme d'Or
1200 Andalucia Avenue
(305) 913-3189

Pascal's on Ponce
2611 Ponce de Leon Boulevard
(305) 444-2024

Pincho Factory
30 Giralda Avenue
(305) 446-5666

Plomo Tequila & Taco Bar
230 Miracle Mile
(305) 456-1928

PokéBao
153 Giralda Avenue
(786) 801-1951

Pummarola Pizzeria
141 Aragon Avenue
(786) 409-6866

Raw Juce
112 Madruga Avenue
(305) 671-3331

Rice Mediterranean Kitchen
164 Giralda Avenu
(305) 200-5282

Sasha's Café
2525 Ponce de Leon
Boulevard
(305) 569-1300

Salumeria 104
117 Miracle Mile

(305) 640-5547

Shula's 347 Grill
6915 South Red Road
(305) 665-9661

Small Tea
205 Aragon Avenue
(786) 401-7189

Spring Chicken
1514 South Dixie Highway
(305) 504-2704

Sushi Maki
2334 Ponce de Leon Boulevard
(305) 443-1884

Taco Rico
473 South Dixie Highway
(305) 663-3200

Talavera
2299 Ponce de Leon Boulevard
(305) 444-2955

The Bar
172 Giralda Avenue
(305) 442-2730

The Globe
377 Alhambra Circle
(305) 445-3555

The Local
150 Giralda Avenue
(305) 648-5687

The Seven Dials
2030 Douglas Road, #102
(786) 542-1603

Threefold Café
141 Giralda Avenue
(305) 704-8007

Tinta y Café
1315 Ponce de Leon Boulevard
(305) 285-0101

Uvaggio
70 Miracle Mile
(305) 448-2400

Veganaroma
3808 SW 8th Street
(305) 444-3826

Whip N Dip
1407 Sunset Drive
(305) 665-2565

Zucca
162 Alcazar Avenue
(786) 580-3731

Recipes Index

Photo Credits

Many of the images appearing in the book were taken by Andrea Mendez, Paola Mendez, Mike Urban, Nabila Verushka and the City of Coral Gables. Many of the other images were provided courtesy of the establishments included in the book.

Other photo credits: page 14, Fiola, Marco Cimmino; pages 18-19: Café at Books & Books and Katie June Burton; page 19: Shutterstock; page 22, top, Shutterstock; page 31, Shutterstock; page 38, Shutterstock; page 39, top, meunierd/ Shutterstock; bottom, Shutterstock; pages 48-49: Vincent Catala Interactive Consulting; page 68, Marco Borghini/Shutterstock; page 69, left, Francisco Bianco/Shutterstock.com; middle, Shutterstock; bottom: courtesy of Fabio and the City of Coral Gables; page 73, Shutterstock; page 75, Shutterstock; page 92, Shutterstock; page 137, Shutterstock

Cover photo credits: upper left, Shutterstock; upper right, courtesy of Kao Sushi & Grill; lower left, courtesy of Bulla Gastrobar; lower right, City of Coral Gables.